SOUND
INVESTING

SOUND INVESTING

UNCOVER FRAUD AND PROTECT YOUR PORTFOLIO

KATE MOONEY
AND
KERRY MARRER

New York   Chicago   San Francisco   Lisbon   London
Madrid   Mexico City   Milan   New Delhi   San Juan   Seoul
Singapore   Sydney   Toronto

ISBN-13: 978-0-07-148182-3
ISBN-10:   0-07-148182-6

McGraw-Hill books are available at special quantity discounts to use as premiums and sales promotions, or for use in corporate training programs. For more information, please write to the Director of Special Sales, Professional Publishing, McGraw-Hill, Two Penn Plaza, New York, NY 10121-2298. Or contact your local bookstore.

To our kids, Aaron and Tim Mooney and Meghan, Sean, and Colin Marrer. Your dynamic spirits make us better people.

CONTENTS

PART III

DETECTING THE TRUTH ON THE INCOME STATEMENT AND STATEMENT OF STOCKHOLDERS' EQUITY

PART IV

UNCOVERING CLUES ON THE BALANCE SHEET

PART V

SPOTTING CLUES IN THE NOTES TO THE FINANCIAL STATEMENTS

PART VI

EVALUATING THE EVIDENCE IN THE ANNUAL REPORT AND SEC FILINGS

ACKNOWLEDGMENTS

This was a challenging undertaking for us, and we struggled with the progress from idea to completed project. Without the support and encouragement of our husbands, Steve Mooney and Jim Marrer, we wouldn't have finished.

A special thanks to Tim Mooney for his work on the EDGAR appendix. Thanks also to Dianne Wheeler and Grace Freedson for the extraordinary patience they exhibited when we stretched deadlines. Finally, Jack Friedman was our first connection to the publishing world and deserves our gratitude.

PART I

THE FINANCIAL ENVIRONMENT— A CRIME SCENE?

CHAPTER 1

THE FINANCIAL PRESSURE

MARKET FORCES AND self-interest tempt chief executive officers (CEOs) and chief financial officers (CFOs) to cross the line from aggressive accounting to fraud. Management is pressured by external forces to show steadily increasing income, to meet forecast earnings, to maintain creditworthiness, and to project the image of a good corporate citizen. Top executives also personally gain from pretty accounting numbers through bonuses and stock options. Companies feel pressure to control reported financial numbers for public relations purposes. The manipulation of accounting numbers to meet desired outcomes brings into question the quality of earnings reported in financial statements.

QUICK POINTS: THE FINANCIAL PRESSURE

Motives for creative accounting include:

❖ The stock market punishes companies that miss the forecasts with decreases in the stock price.
❖ Violation of debt covenants that specify minimum ratios using accounting numbers can require refinancing at higher rates.
❖ Executive compensation is dependent on meeting certain measures based on accounting numbers.

Why Are Executives Willing to Take the Risk?

Executives have many motives for perpetrating financial farces. Most of those motives are related to investment, credit, and compensation transactions. Economic events such as market trading prices, borrowing terms, and bonus awards are determined by the numbers on the financial statements or how those numbers relate to expectations.

Market Punishment

CEOs are under pressure to maximize shareholder value. Fail at that, and shareholders will be looking for another leader. As a result, managers maximize shareholder value by managing the business in a way that increases the stock price. A look at the *Wall Street Journal*, and readers are clued in to one cause of increased stock price: strong earnings. While the dot-com businesses of the 1990s are an exception to the rule, established companies do not want to report losses.

According to the *Wall Street Journal* (November 10, 2006), HealthSouth Corporation's stock fell to its lowest level after the company announced a larger third-quarter loss in November 2006. The market punishes companies that report losses with large decreases in stock price, so the executive is motivated to report income, not losses, even if it takes some creative methods of accounting to achieve that outcome.

Another way to increase stock price is through steadily, slowly increasing earnings over time, each period showing slightly better results than the previous one. Top managers feel the pressure to prevent surprises in reported earnings. The goal is a pattern of income that is slowly but steadily increasing. This model of earnings makes it easier to predict future performance, reducing the risk of the investment as perceived by analysts or investors. The market rewards a company that exhibits slow, steady earnings growth over a long period of time with increasing stock prices, and managers will take measures to smooth income to get those rewards. Coca-Cola and McDonald's are examples of companies whose earnings have been slow and steady. In reaction to that, their stock prices have been steadily climbing. Other companies, such as Chrysler, have had erratic earnings that likewise cause erratic stock prices.

Along with the pressure to report income rather than loss and the pressure to make that a gently increasing income, a third source of pressure for managers is the pressure to meet the earnings expectations. Missing the forecast, even by a very small amount, brings a strong reprimand in the form of reduced stock price. Dell, Inc., the personal computer maker, announced in May 2006 that its quarterly profit missed the company's forecast, causing its shares to drop 6 percent. Both JC Penney and Costco Wholesale had increases in sales in November 2006, but the increases did not meet Wall Street's expectations, which in turn caused their stock to fall. To avoid that decline in value, executives will manage the earnings to just meet the forecast. Often that involves pushing earnings up. However, it may also involve deflating earnings, out of fear that future periods won't be able to sustain the current period's earnings.

And just meeting the forecast is not always enough. The stock price also goes down if earnings don't exceed the forecast number by as much as expected, further motivating managers to inflate income through accounting choices.

Market factors motivate top executives to manage earnings to either avoid losses, continue slow and steady growth, or meet expectations. The failure to manage earnings to accomplish these goals results in decreased stock prices, unhappy investors, and deterioration of the executive's reputation. That could mean job loss for the manager. Avoiding unemployment is a powerful motivator.

Creditor Punishment

In addition to the pressure to maintain or increase stock prices, managers are under pressure to maintain or increase the creditworthiness of the company. The company's credit rating affects two things: first, the slack in existing debt covenants, and second, the cost and amount of new borrowing.

Managers must comply with the restrictions that lenders place on them as a condition of the borrowing. Debt covenants establish benchmarks for ratios relating to cash and additional borrowing. The restrictions serve to reduce the risk of non-repayment and take the form of thresholds for certain ratios and limits on additional debt.

If a company is not in compliance with the restrictions, the lender can waive the violation or require refinancing at a higher rate. Although a waiver does not have immediate cash consequences, it can still cause difficulties, both real and perceived. Real difficulties occur because lenders rarely allow multiple waivers. So using a waiver in the current year leaves the company fewer alternatives and less flexibility in the future. Waivers, which are included in financial reports, are perceived as a signal of financial problems. The result is lower stock prices.

For example, Expedia Inc.'s stock price fell after it was spun off from IAC/InterActive Corp. in 2005. This leads to the possibility that Expedia will have to write off some of the goodwill on its balance sheet. This write-off would cause stockholders' equity to decline and may lead to Expedia's being in violation of a debt covenant.

CEOs and CFOs are motivated to manipulate the numbers to meet the required ratio thresholds and avoid market declines associated with credit problems. While existing loan covenants are motivators for creative accounting, maintaining the company's ability to borrow in the future is another.

The company may need debt financing to take advantage of a future opportunity, and the interest rate charged is dependent on the credit rating of the company, which is based on repayment history and earnings. Higher earnings also support higher borrowing limits, giving the company the chance to take on more new projects with high returns but that require borrowing. To get more favorable debt terms, including a lower interest cost and higher loan limit, executives will choose accounting rules that present results most favorably.

External forces are important reasons why executives take the risk and choose aggressive accounting methods. They choose methods to manage the earnings to expectations or to meet debt requirements to avoid punishment from the stock market or creditors. In addition to the external forces, though, internal motivators also exist.

Self-Interest

While executives use creative accounting methods to maximize shareholder value, not all the motives are so altruistic. Those same executives have self-interests in the reported financial numbers. Bonuses are usually dependent on meeting or exceeding certain thresholds. Top management feels the pressure to target those thresholds but not to exceed them by much, so as to save those earnings for the next bonus year. Management is motivated to use aggressive or creative accounting to manipulate the earnings number so that their own wealth is maximized, too, by just meeting the bonus target every year.

In addition to their interest in bonus thresholds, executives may also have stock options. The value of a stock option to the holder of the option is the difference between the option price and the market price of the stock. So, while executives are increasing stock price to help shareholders receive a bigger return through appreciation, those same activities also benefit the holders of stock options, providing a bigger positive difference between the option price and the market price of the stock. Many executives receive stock options as part of their compensation, so many executives are motivated to report numbers that will increase the stock price, especially during the exercise period of the options.

Political Pressure

While executives feel economic pressure to produce earnings that represent a desired level of performance for economic reasons, top-level managers are also exposed to another pressure—political pressure. This is political pressure not just in the sense of that coming from Democrats or Republicans—although legislators are happy to get involved if it will win favor with voters—but in the public's perception of the company. Corporations with huge profits are considered greedy, especially when the profits come at the pain of ordinary citizens. Angry, dissatisfied citizens contact their government and demand action. Federal, state, and local governments respond to citizens' requests for them to "do something" about high gas prices, monopolies, or the problem du jour with legislation or regulation that adds costs to doing business. Managers may actually manage earnings down to avoid these costs. Current industries or companies that are under this spotlight are oil companies and pharmaceutical companies. Microsoft, specifically, is constantly being watched because of its perceived monopoly.

The financial and economic environment in which company managers operate is filled with pressures to report earnings in a way that increases the stock price, increases the creditworthiness of the company, and increases their own personal wealth. The social environment puts political pressure on managers to avoid negative perceptions by the public.

Earnings Management

With all the pressure, what do managers do? They manage, of course. In fact, they even manage earnings. They do this by choosing certain techniques or by making estimates in a way that produces the desired numbers.

Not all management of earnings is fraudulent or deceptive. In many instances, the inherent flexibility of accounting rules, the use of estimates, and the judgment required in financial reporting are necessary to accommodate different industries, forms of business, and environments. The question is, when does the implementation of choices, estimates, and judgment move from acceptable to fraudulent and deceptive? When are the choices, estimates, and judgments so slanted that the numbers on the financial statements are distorted? These questions relate to the quality of earnings.

Quality of Earnings

The quality of earnings is measured on the basis of how closely the reported earnings numbers reflect the economic reality. High-quality earnings closely reflect the real performance of the company. High-quality earnings provide decision makers with information about future levels and patterns of income. If the current period's earnings are improved by selected accounting methods, then the future level of earnings is misrepresented, leading to poorer investment and credit decisions and overcompensation through bonuses to employees. If the current period's earnings are smoothed, reducing the variability, creditors could make bad judgments about sustained repayment capability.

It would seem that the less manipulation of earnings through aggressive accounting choices, the better the information about firm performance would be. The key is determining how much manipulation is being done.

THE OPPORTUNITY

MOTIVATION ISN'T THE only condition necessary for managers to perpetrate a financial farce. The opportunity must exist. With all the laws and regulations, plus the accounting rules, it is hard to imagine that the opportunity to manipulate earnings is present.

QUICK POINTS: THE OPPORTUNITY

- ❖ Research results prove that accounting numbers are manipulated.
- ❖ Three reasons why it is possible to use creative accounting are:
  - ❖ Accounting standards are flexible.
  - ❖ Business transactions are complex.
  - ❖ Controls are either weak or not enforced.

Can You Prove That the Opportunity Exists?

Yes, researchers have found proof. Academics using large databases of accounting and stock price information have found some interesting patterns indicating that managers utilize techniques to decrease and increase reported earnings.

You would expect that the size of losses and profits would be random over thousands of quarterly earnings numbers reported over decades. But researchers have found that the number of small losses reported on financial statements is unusually small. In other words, most reported losses are big. Statistics suggest that this is not by chance, which means managers, realizing the company is going to record a loss for the period, decide to include any discretionary negative items into the calculation. So, searching through the books for discretionary items, a company might decide now is the time to unload that loser stock investment, or sell that odd property at a loss, or write off that obsolete inventory—all actions that decrease earnings. The logic is that the company will be punished with a lower stock price for a loss, regardless of the size of the loss. By finalizing anything that might possibly reduce income, including it in this year's loss, and taking the hit to the stock price this year, the company might be able to save itself from a small loss in the future that would also reduce the stock price. Managers believe they are avoiding a future market punishment by taking all the bad things into income now.

Researchers have also found an unusually large number of small reported profits. A possible explanation is that managers manipulate earnings just enough to move into the profit range. Recognizing that less manipulation will be harder to detect and that presenting a small profit will be less suspicious, managers move earnings only as far as necessary, not dramatically.

Studying those databases reveals patterns other than big losses and small profits. Researchers have found evidence of maneuvering by managers to sustain a trend. The change in earnings from one year to the next is an important signal. A small, consistent increase is viewed positively because it indicates continued earnings growth. Intuitively, though, you would expect that a company's earnings would increase a little over the previous period, just about as often as the earnings would decrease slightly. It seems unlikely that complex corporations with operations all over the globe could sustain a constant, small growth rate over years with differing oil prices, taxes, and international crises. The research shows, however, that a small decrease in earnings is a rare event, but a small increase is common. This nonrandom pattern suggests some action is at work that produces the unusual number of small increases in earnings.

Why Does the Opportunity Exist?

The opportunity to manipulate earnings exists for three reasons:

1. Accounting standards are flexible.
2. Business transactions are complex.
3. Controls to prevent the behavior are weak.

These reasons are part of the business environment and are hard to eliminate.

Opportunity #1: Flexible Accounting Standards

By design, accounting standards are flexible. The Financial Accounting Standards Board (FASB) sets the rules that businesses must follow when doing their accounting and producing their financial statements. Setting the rules is a complicated activity that must take into consideration many different kinds of businesses and many different kinds of transactions. It is impossible to make a rule for every economic event. So the FASB crafts guidelines that apply to a generalized situation, leaving flexibility in application to present better financial information based on the specific facts surrounding the event. Finding the right balance of detail and generalization is difficult. If the rules are too detailed, businesses find it easy to meet the letter of the rule, but get around the spirit of it. On the other hand, establishing rules that are based on principles, instead of prescriptive procedures, means that the manager has to use judgment in applying the rules to a particular business event. The flexibility to use judgment gives the manager the opportunity to manage earnings because some alternatives may produce a more desired outcome.

For example, imagine a situation in which a business leases a building for its operations. The lease is structured in such a way that at the end of the lease the title to the building passes automatically to the lessee. Obviously, this is a transaction that is called a lease, but it is really a purchase and the lease payments are really loan payments. To achieve the goal of having all debt presented in the financial statements, a prescriptive accounting rule would require the lessee to record any lease in which title transfers automatically at the end of the lease as a financed purchase. That would involve listing the debt on the balance sheet, giving financial statement readers information about the obligations of the company. Investors generally prefer to buy stock in companies that have less debt rather than more debt, so this information about the financed purchase might make the stock less desirable and, therefore, the stock price lower.

It would be easy for the company to get around the rule by setting up the lease to give the lessee the option to buy the building at the end of the lease . . . for $1. In that case, since the lessee did not automatically take title to the building but had to buy it, there would be no need to record the debt. The only term that is different in the transaction is the $1 paid at the end, but the accounting is very different. Because the transfer of title was not automatic, the company would not need to put the obligation on the balance sheet, thereby looking "better" to investors because it showed less debt.

A more general accounting rule would require recording all purchases involving loans in the financial statements, regardless of the language used to name the transaction. The company's managers would have to look at the transaction and determine whether the characteristics were those of a purchase with a loan or a lease. Without specific rules or precise measures, managers would have to interpret the rules for each situation and use judgment to determine the proper accounting. Managers would have to decide whether the contract specifications were more like a lease or more like a purchase funded by a loan and then choose which way to do the accounting based on their interpretation.

The necessity of using judgment could lead to the opportunity for manipulation of earnings.

Not all judgment calls produce financial farces as obvious as the lease example. Instead, interpretations of accounting rules are on a continuum from conservative to aggressive to illegal. But the line between aggressive and illegal is not always perfectly clear.

Opportunity #2: Complex Business Transactions

Both globalization and technology have provided the impetus and the means for complex transactions. New international markets require new methods, and small, high-speed computers provide the ability to do many intricate calculations quickly. Ambitious managers trying to increase firm value through higher stock price are regularly developing new ways of doing business.

Resourceful business executives, with advice from accountants and lawyers, are constantly inventing new and different techniques to accomplish business goals. One type of technique involves creative ways of financing. An example is securitization of existing receivables. Companies sell the rights to receive the payments on amounts owed to them and charge a servicing fee to manage the payments. Many lenders do this with their mortgage loans. The accounting problem involves determining what exactly was sold. Was it the rights to receive the payments or was it the actual receivables? If the transaction structure does not meet the very detailed requirements of certain accounting rules, then the receivables are really still owned by the selling company. This means that those assets remain on the seller's books, reducing the return on assets, an important measure of how efficiently a company can produce income from its assets.

If, on the other hand, the transaction does qualify as a sale, then the seller can record a gain or loss on the income statement and, because the assets are not included in the financial ratios, the return on assets improves. Companies prefer the sale treatment because it can provide them with an increase in income through a gain on the sale and a better measure of performance through a higher return on assets. Managers take advantage of the complexities to contrive a sale of the receivables.

Another set of complicated business techniques involves new types of relationships such as special-purpose entities. Companies can use special-purpose entities to hold financed assets so that neither the debt nor the asset appears on the company's books. The catch is, though, that those special-purpose entities cannot be controlled by the company. With less recorded debt, the company's ratios look better and the company has the flexibility to use additional debt in the future. With fewer assets, the company's return on assets is better. So the goal for management is to somehow make it look like the company is not controlling a special-purpose entity that owns the assets used by the company. Setting up a transaction that meets the requirements for the preferred treatment is tricky, because of the confusing requirements, but it's worth the trouble because companies prefer to have assets and the associated debt off their balance sheet and on the books of the special-purpose entity.

A third type of technique involves methods of managing risk. Examples of sophisticated risk reduction include derivatives and hedging transactions. Managers use both to offset possible losses from changes in interest rates, prices, and currency valuation. When used properly and understood correctly, derivatives and hedges offset unforeseen changes in value, thereby protecting the entity from big losses or big gains. However, these transactions don't always work perfectly, and the accounting for the change in value that is not controlled by the hedge or derivative is difficult to comprehend.

Understanding a complex set of business exchanges, contracts, or relationships takes lots of expertise and intelligence. The auditor who examines the books must have that expertise to make certain the accounting is honest and represents the reality of the deal.

But acquiring that proficiency is difficult. That level of expertise and understanding is expensive to acquire and takes time to apply to specific situations, eventually resulting in higher audit fees. Continuing professional education courses, required to remain an active certified public accountant (CPA), evolve *after* the techniques are in use, so auditors have no specific guidance for investigating the latest financial innovation.

The creativity of business executives and the complexity of new transactions that are difficult to understand and audit provide businesses with the opportunity to manipulate earnings.

Opportunity #3: Weak Controls

Managers can manipulate the reported financial numbers because the controls that are supposed to prevent that activity are weak or altogether lacking. Internal control is the accounting lingo for the system inside a business that prevents anyone—employee, executive, or outsider—from tampering with the valuables of the business, including assets and information. The internal control system should prescribe how things are done and who does them, plus somehow document that the rules are followed. To prevent fraudulent financial reporting, internal control processes should be in place to ensure that the financial reporting is reliable and follows accounting rules.

Unfortunately, though, internal control systems have design problems and enforcement problems. Designing a system to eliminate fraud is impossible because the cost would be total inefficiency. So the company has an internal control system that is a compromise between control and efficiency and, admittedly, only deters but is not 100 percent effective at preventing fraud. Added to that inherent weakness are the situations in which even the existing controls are not enforced, so it is easy to understand how fraudulent reporting happens.

Section 404 of the Sarbanes-Oxley Act should improve this situation. It requires the management of large publicly traded companies to issue a report on the internal control over financial reporting as part of the company's Securities and Exchange Commission (SEC) report. The auditors then report on management's report. This increased attention to the internal control over financial reporting should help eliminate some of the opportunity for fraudulent financial reporting for the very largest corporations.

Unfortunately, this aspect of the Sarbanes-Oxley Act affects only very large companies that sell stock to the public—those companies valued at $75 million or more. And even more unfortunately, the SEC has delayed the extension of the internal control reporting requirement for any companies smaller than the existing threshold.

Although it seems all the laws and rules are in place to prevent it, companies still find ways to manipulate the results displayed on their financial statements. Researchers have found that the pattern of income and losses doesn't follow normal statistical models, implying that those numbers are not occurring naturally but are contrived. The opportunity to engage in actions that present earnings numbers in the most advantageous way is explained by the flexibility of accounting standards, the complexity of transactions, and the difficulty of designing and enforcing effective controls to prevent fiddling with the numbers.

CHAPTER 3

THE RATIONALIZATION

HUMAN BEINGS FIND it hard to accept their own guilt, and corporate fraudsters are no exception. Even when indicted, executives charged with fraud maintain their innocence. Bernard Ebbers, the former chief executive of WorldCom Inc., maintained his innocence after being sentenced to 25 years in prison for his part in the WorldCom fraud. When former Enron CEO Jeffrey Skilling was sentenced to 24 years in prison for his part in the fall of Enron, he maintained his innocence also. It appears that rationalization is a key component of the fraud. The perpetrators must justify their actions. The rationalization can justify the fraud because it helps others or because it really is not a wrongful act.

QUICK POINTS: THE RATIONALIZATION

Rationalizations for aggressive or fraudulent accounting include:

❖ We were protecting the shareholders.
❖ We were protecting the jobs of the employees.
❖ We'll make it up next period.
❖ I deserve it.

Rationalization #1: This Action Is Necessary to Protect the Shareholders from Steep Declines in Stock Prices, so It Isn't Really Wrong

The executives who commit fraud often maintain that they are really doing it for the shareholders or employees. The logic is that if the accounting manipulation does not "fix" the numbers, then the stock price will decline. That decline in stock price will hurt the shareholders. The executive can protect the shareholders from this decline in stock price by doing whatever it takes to meet the required target. If the target is an earnings target, the manager can speed up revenue recognition, delay expenses, or manage some reserve amounts. If the target is a debt level, the manager will arrange for off-balance-sheet debt, the kind that does not appear in the financial statements. The rationalization is that the actions are taken to protect shareholders from declines in value, which neutralizes the bad aspect of the fraud. It was done for the right reasons.

Rationalization #2: It Isn't Really Bad Because I'm Doing It to Protect the Employees from Losing Their Jobs

A similar rationalization involves committing the fraud to protect the employees. In this case, the executive believes that if the accounting numbers are not "fixed," the company might lay off workers, or, in the worst case, the company might go out of business, resulting in job loss for all employees. By fudging the numbers, the fraudster will keep the employees from losing their livelihood and their retirement savings. This logic makes the fraudulent actions acceptable because it is for the benefit of the employees.

Rationalization #3: We Can Make This Up Next Period and No One Will Ever Know

Although some fraudsters rationalize their actions as really doing good for shareholders and employees, other rationalizations make the act itself seem not wrong. Many times, accounting fraud involves recognizing revenue before it is really earned. For example, if the sales revenue is a little below the target for the period, the company might offer special terms that entice customers to buy before the end of the period. The terms might include deep discounts or generous return privileges. Or sales taking place just shortly *after* the cutoff for the period are really included as if they occurred just *before* the end. The fraudsters who use these techniques fool themselves into thinking that they can make it up in the next period. Because the sales actually exist and just need a little adjusting to get them into the right time period, the fraudster rationalizes that the actions are not really wrong. The problem, though, is that often the company needs to make up not only the amount from the previous period but also the shortfall for the current period. That initial underperformance was really a signal of declining revenue, and the amount to make up just keeps getting bigger.

Rationalization #4: I'm Underpaid and Underappreciated, So I Really Deserve the Reward That Results from Manipulating the Numbers

Probably the least sympathetic rationalization is the "I deserve it" justification. In the mind of the fraudsters, they deserve whatever it is they are getting as a result of their fraud, and that puts it within acceptable limits. They think of themselves as saving a floundering business, so they deserve all the perks that go with the reputation of a corporate magician. They may also rationalize that they have earned the compensation associated with their stock options, so they will do whatever is necessary to maximize the value of those options. The entitlement rationale is based on greed—greed for the lifestyle associated with a corporate executive or greed for the compensation dollars associated with the increased value of stock options.

The people who perpetrate financial fraud often use rationalizations to make it palatable to themselves. Those rationalizations range from saving the jobs of employees and preserving the wealth of shareholders to entitlement.

PART II

BACKGROUND, THEORIES, AND CONCEPTS THAT FORM THE FRAMEWORK OF ACCOUNTING

CHAPTER 4

REVENUE RECOGNITION

ON THE SURFACE, it should be easy—you make the sale, then you record the revenue. The question is, how do you determine *when* the sale was made—that is, the exact moment in time? That timing is important. For some companies, including the dollars from a sale in this month's revenue number will make the difference between meeting the earnings forecast and missing it (and missing the forecast can bring severe consequences).

QUICK POINTS: REVENUE RECOGNITION

- ✧ If a company recognizes revenue, that means that dollar amount can be included on the current-period income statement.
- ✧ Current accounting rules provide for revenue recognition when two things happen:
  - ✧ Payment is likely or has occurred.
  - ✧ Goods are delivered.
- ✧ Revenue recognition is complicated when services are the product being sold.
- ✧ Variations of revenue recognition rules exist that affect the timing of the recognition.
- ✧ New revenue recognition rules will focus on the changes in assets and liabilities on the balance sheet.
- ✧ A company must disclose the revenue recognition methods used in the notes to the financial statements.

Current Accounting Rules

The Financial Accounting Standards Board, the group in charge of making accounting rules, issued the Statement of Financial Accounting Concepts No. 5, which provides guidance for recognizing revenue. Revenue should be included on the period's income statement when cash is received or it is likely that cash will be received. This usually occurs when the company has delivered the goods or provided services.

Let's examine how this definition works, using some sales transactions. In setup 1, a couple goes to an appliance store and buys a refrigerator that is on the showroom floor, paying $2,000 in cash and loading it on their truck. That's easy. The store has realized the cash and given up the refrigerator. The revenue is included in the month's sales.

Setup 2 is similar, except the customers don't pay cash; instead, they agree to pay for the refrigerator in installments over the next six months. Assuming the customers are a good credit risk, the store is likely to receive the cash and the refrigerator has been given to the buyers, so the store can include the revenue in the current period's revenue.

Setup 3 gets more complicated because now, instead of finding a refrigerator on the sales floor, the customers order one and pay 10 percent down, agreeing to pay the remainder when the refrigerator is delivered. In this situation, the correct revenue recognition choice depends on the precise situation. If for any reason the customers lose the down payment, even if the refrigerator isn't delivered, then the store can recognize revenue up to the amount of the down payment, which is $200. If the customers would get a refund for the down payment in some circumstances, then no revenue is recognized. Instead, an obligation, or liability, is set up for the amount of the down payment. In neither case, though, is the full price of the refrigerator included in revenue. The delivery of the refrigerator determines when that happens.

Dealing with a tangible product, the refrigerator, that is delivered all at one time makes the timing of revenue recognition an easier target. The company can actually determine when the ownership of the product changed hands. Revenue recognition becomes messy when the "product" is a service provided over time as part of the sale, such as technical support, with no precise measure of quantity or cost. The timing and amount of revenue recognition in that case requires considerable judgment. Suppose that, in addition to the refrigerator, the company sells an extended warranty on the refrigerator that extends the manufacturer's warranty of one year by two additional years. The cost is $100. Determining when to recognize the $100 of revenue is complicated and depends on when it is earned. It should be recognized in the future over the time period covered by the extension.

Another complication involves return guarantees. If the refrigerator store allows customers to return an appliance within 30 days for a full refund, the store really hasn't earned the revenue until after the 30 days expire. Figure 4.1 illustrates these examples.

Figure 4.1

Example	*Date of Revenue Recognition*
1. 6/15 Customer purchases $2,000 refrigerator for cash and takes it home.	6/15 Record $2,000 sales revenue.
2. 6/15 Customer purchases $2,000 refrigerator, agrees to pay in installments, and takes it home.	6/15 Record $2,000 sales revenue.
3. 6/15 Customer orders refrigerator with $200 down payment (nonrefundable).	6/15 Record $200 sales revenue. Date of delivery, record $1,800 sales revenue.
4. 6/15 Customer orders refrigerator with $200 down payment (refundable).	6/15 Record $200 liability. Date of delivery, record $2,000 revenue and eliminate liability.
Effect of 30-Day Right to Return	
Examples 1 and 2	30 days after delivery, record $2,000 sales revenue.
Example 3	6/15 Record $200 sales revenue. 30 days after delivery, record additional $1,800 sales revenue.
Example 4	6/15 Record $200 liability. 30 days after delivery, record $2,000 sales revenue and eliminate $200 liability.

Variations of Revenue Recognition Methods

The percentage-of-completion method of revenue recognition is a variation of the payment likely–product delivered, or sales basis method, described previously. This method is used for long-term contracts and recognizes revenue before the project is complete. Aircraft companies use this method and actually include revenue from building a plane before the plane is complete. To implement the percentage-of-completion method, the company must be able to use a logical process to estimate how much of the contract has been fulfilled. The most common method is to compare the costs so far to the total estimated costs and calculate the percentage of the contract that is complete. In step 2, that percentage is applied to the total revenue or total gross profit of the contract to determine how much revenue or profit should be recognized to this point in the contract. In step 3, to get the current period's amount, the previously recognized revenue, or profit, is subtracted from the amount in step 2. If the contract is going to result in a loss, the entire loss is included on the income statement as soon as it is known that a loss will occur.

The percentage-of-completion method is common in some industries, but it can be manipulated. If the company wants to increase the amount of revenue recognized, it only has to load up on raw materials and use the costs of materials purchased, rather than those used, to inflate the revenue. Even if the estimate of completion is based on materials used, it still results in an earlier recognition of revenue than the sales basis method.

Let's look at a simple example. Assume a contractor agrees to construct a building for $5,000,000. The building will take approximately three years to complete. The total costs of the building are estimated to be $4,000,000. In year 1, the contractor incurs $1,000,000 in costs. The revenue that will be recognized in year 1 under the percentage-of-completion method is $1,250,000 ($1,000,000/$4,000,000 × $5,000,000). If the contractor loaded up on $500,000 of raw materials at the end of the year and included those costs in the calculations, the revenue to be recognized would increase to $1,875,000 ($1,500,000/$4,000,000 × $5,000,000).

The installment method of recognizing revenue is used when payments are received over time and collection of those payments is not certain. This method puts off the recognition of profit to the point of collection. When making an installment method sale, the company calculates the percentage of profit from the sale. That percentage is then applied to the amount of cash collections to calculate the amount of profit to recognize. If interest is part of the cash collections, that part of the payments has to be accounted for as interest income.

Using the previous $5,000,000 building example, the profit on this contract would be $1,000,000 or 20 percent. Assume the customer makes a payment of $1,500,000 the first year after completion and will be paying the remainder the next year. The contractor would recognize $300,000 of profit under the installment method ($1,500,000 × .20) in the year of the first payment and $700,000 (3,500,000 × .20) the year of the second payment.

The cost recovery method of revenue recognition is very conservative and does not recognize any revenue until the amount of the payments received covers all the expenses from the product. This method of revenue recognition is usually used when payment for the sale is received over a long period of time and the likelihood of collection is unknown and undeterminable. All cash collections are first applied to the cost of the product sold. After that amount has been collected, the seller recognizes profit.

In the preceding building example, the contractor would not recognize any profit until the $4,000,000 in costs had been recovered. If the contractor received a payment of $1,500,000, that same amount of revenue would be recognized along with the same amount of expenses, resulting in no profit for the year.

New Revenue Recognition Rules

The FASB plans on changing the rules for revenue recognition in 2007. The Revenue Recognition Project may significantly modify the existing guidelines. Those modifications, though, will not affect the basic model of revenue recognition in which revenue is recognized in the current period's income statement when the product is delivered and payment is received or likely to be received. Instead, the adjustments will affect more complicated business models in which rights to receive something or obligations to perform are bought and sold. The amount of revenue will be determined by the amount of change in assets and liabilities, not the earnings process and payment.

For example, considering the aforementioned refrigerator example, revenue would depend on the amount received for the refrigerator and the extended warranty and the value of the extension of the warranty. If the refrigerator store could buy a contract that would perform the warranty work for $45, then the revenue from the transaction would be the increase in cash of $2,000 less the value of the liability to perform the warranty work of $45, or $1,955. The key to using this method is having market values for all the products or services.

Disclosure of Revenue Recognition Methods

So how do you know which method of revenue recognition is used by the companies in your portfolio? They must tell you, and they do that through the notes to the financial statements. If you have an actual annual report, you will find that disclosure in the very first note.

You can also check this out on the Internet for almost any company by doing a Google search at www.google.com. In the search box, type the name of a company and the words "annual report." For example, try using an IBM annual report. The search for "IBM annual report" results in one that actually says

"IBM 2004 Annual Report." If you click on that item, you are taken to a page that allows you to download a copy of the report or to search it. If you search for "revenue recognition," the results will take you to the first note on significant accounting policies, which includes disclosure of IBM's revenue recognition methods. Every publicly traded company must disclose its revenue recognition method in the first note to the annual report on significant accounting policies.

Revenues Are Different from Gains

Not all positive amounts on the income statement are revenues. Gains are another type of positive dollar amount on the income statement. The effect of gains and revenues on income is the same. Both increase the amount of profit, but the distinction is important for your understanding of the company's future business performance. Gains are positive amounts that are not related to the normal business operations. A gain could be something like the result of a retail store selling a property at a price higher than the cost of that property. Revenues, on the other hand, are the result of the sales of the company's regular products or services. This differentiation gives readers of the income statement a better idea of the income that will continue in the future. With that information, readers can assess the profitability and success of the core operations of the business and not be confused by one-time increases. Clearly, a retail business that consistently increases income through the sale of store properties will eventually have no stores left in which to make sales.

CHAPTER 5

COST ALLOCATION

Expense recognition in the business world is very different from expense recognition in personal finance. This means that a transaction doesn't become an expense on the income statement for the period just because the company wrote a check for that amount during the period. Instead, recognizing expenses often depends on the particular revenues that have been recognized. Like revenues, the timing issue affects the matched expenses. Companies that are just short of the forecast earnings have an incentive to delay expense recognition. Companies that have greatly exceeded forecast earnings have the incentive to recognize all the expenses possible, thereby saving a future shortfall

---

QUICK POINTS: COST ALLOCATION

- In the accounting world, expenses are different from costs, from expenditures, and from tax deductions.
- Costs may be stored on the balance sheet until it is time to include them on the income statement.
- Companies use several methods of determining which expenses must be included on the current period's income statement.
- Matching is the most common method of cost allocation.
- Systematic allocation of cost is an acceptable means of recognizing expenses.
- Some types of expenses are so susceptible to manipulation that very precise rules govern the recognition of them.
- Expenses are different from losses.

---

through early recognition of expenses. The trick is to figure a way to recognize both the right amount of revenue and the right amount of expenses.

The Words Make a Difference

Businesses use precise language when it comes to expenses. *Expenditures, costs,* and *expenses* all mean different things. Expenditures are transactions for which the company has made a payment. Businesses buy inventory, pay salaries, and purchase equipment and buildings, and all those are expenditures. The actual transaction is the expenditure. But expenditures made during a particular period may or may not be recognized as expenses on that accounting period's income statement.

Costs are the result of past expenditures. Costs are dollar amounts that are waiting to be recognized as expenses in a particular accounting period. A cost is usually stored on the balance sheet as an asset if the item purchased will be used for more than one accounting period. For example, a company buys a building. The purchase transaction is the expenditure for a building. The cost, or purchase amount, is on the balance sheet as an asset. The cost of the building is recognized as an expense on income statements over the period of time during which the building is used by the company. Expenses are negative amounts on the income statement; they reduce net income. Expenses are often the result of expenditures but can sometimes be estimates of pending expenditures. The rules for including expenses on an income statement for a particular time period are different from the rules for including deductions on the company's tax return. Not all expenses are tax deductible. In addition to nondeductibility, some expenses that are tax deductible may be measured differently for tax purposes, making the deductible amount different from the expense amount. The key is to realize that in business, expenditures, costs, expenses, and tax deductions are not synonyms.

Methods of Allocating Cost

Most expenses are recognized using one of two methods: matching or a systematic allocation. Matching is the most common method of recognizing expenses, and it depends on the revenue that is recognized. The matching principle says that businesses first determine the revenues that will be included on the period's income statement. Then, all the costs of generating those revenues are matched and recognized on the same income statement. For example, if a business recognizes the revenue from selling a couch to a customer on an income statement, on that same income statement it should include an expense for the cost of that couch from the supplier.

Matching sounds easy, but it can be complicated and require some judgments and estimates. In the couch example, it is easy to determine the cost that should be recognized as an expense. But generating revenue includes many more costs, such as those for a building, office equipment, utilities, and insurance. When precise matching isn't possible, a systematic allocation of the cost is the best method to use.

Systematic allocation requires judgment to develop a scheme for recognizing costs as expenses. For example, to recognize the cost of a building, a portion of the cost of the building is recognized as an expense on every income statement during the time the business is using the building. That systematic allocation of building cost is called *depreciation*, and accounting rules prescribe several different schemes for calculating it. Many systematic allocation schemes are based on the passage of time. Another example of a systematic allocation is commonly used for equipment and vehicles. The business makes an estimate of the total number of units the equipment will produce or miles the vehicle will drive. Then, during the accounting period, the actual number of units or miles is recorded. That percentage of the cost is recognized as the expense for the period. Systematic allocation is based on estimates and judgment.

Exceptions to the Cost Allocation Rules

Accounting rules have identified some costs that are susceptible to manipulation because the estimates are difficult to make and prescribes very specific ways to account for those expenses. For example, advertising costs are expensed as soon as the first ad in the series runs. Deviating from that rule requires special justification and is not common. Another example is the costs of research and development activities. These costs are usually recognized as expenses as soon as they are paid, and they are not matched with whatever is being developed. There are some exceptions for when a company may capitalize the research and development costs if the project is at an advanced stage. Such exceptions allow flexibility and require management judgment, which may lead to earnings manipulation.

Expenses Are Different from Losses

Not all negative amounts on the income statement are expenses. Losses are another type of negative dollar amount on the income statement. The effect of losses and the effect of expenses on income are the same. Both reduce the amount of profit. But the distinction is important for your understanding of the company's future business performance. Losses are negative amounts that are not related to the normal business operations. Losses could be things like the costs associated with disposing of a truck that was in a serious accident or the costs of flood damage in excess of insurance. Expenses, on the other hand, are the normal costs of doing business. This differentiation gives readers of the income statement a better idea of the expenses that will continue in the future. With this information, readers can assess the profitability and success of the core operations of the business and not be confused by one-time charges.

Revenues and expenses are the major components of the income statement. In Chapter 6, we move to the balance sheet and delve into the process of measuring the elements found on that financial statement.

VALUATION OF ASSETS AND LIABILITIES

SEVERAL DIFFERENT METHODS exist for measuring the value of assets and liabilities. The method used depends on the nature of the asset or liability. Accounting rules specify what a company must use to measure the value of items on its balance sheet.

QUICK POINTS: VALUATION OF ASSETS AND LIABILITIES

- ✧ Assets on the balance sheet can be valued at:
  - ✧ Historical cost.
  - ✧ Market value.
  - ✧ Lower of cost or market value.
  - ✧ Net realizable value.
  - ✧ Impairment testing.
- ✧ Liabilities on the balance sheet can be valued at:
  - ✧ Cash required to settle the obligation.
  - ✧ Present value of the cash flows required to settle the obligation.
- ✧ You can use the balance sheet values to analyze investments by calculating various ratios.

Asset Valuation Methods

Following are descriptions of the various methods used in asset valuation.

Historical Cost

The most common way of measuring the value of assets is to use the actual cost of the asset. Called *historical cost*, this method simply inserts the dollar amount paid for the asset as the balance sheet value and is easily applied to things like property and vehicles. As we discussed in Chapter 5, for assets used for more than one year, such as buildings, equipment, and vehicles, the historical cost is the dollar amount that is then allocated to depreciation expense over the period of use.

Although historical cost is easy to apply and provides a good measure for some assets, it isn't always an informative measure of value for every kind of asset. Imagine a business that bought the land for the company headquarters in Manhattan in 1926. That land is valued at the 1926 purchase price on the 2006 balance sheet, which would be significantly less than the current market value. But because of the expense of an annual appraisal, the historical cost method is used for land, even though it is not particularly informative.

Market Value

Some assets, however, are measured at their market value. This method is used for measuring the value of investments. On the balance sheet, investments are valued at the current market price. For many stock investments, that value is easy to find because it is published in the *Wall Street Journal*. The current market value of the investment tells the reader of the financial statements how much cash the company could raise by selling the investment.

Lower of Cost or Market

Not all assets have values that increase; some decrease. Therefore, some assets are measured at a value that is the lower of the cost of the asset or the market value of the asset. This method of asset valuation is applied to inventory and provides good information about the salability of the inventory. In most retail situations, a store needs up-to-date merchandise to entice customers to buy. The inventory of goods to sell becomes harder to sell as it ages. For example, think of an electronics store that in 2001 bought many computers for resale. But economic conditions resulted in decreased demand, and 80 of these computers are in the warehouse still waiting to be sold. Obviously, that inventory doesn't have the most current features and is going to be difficult to sell without a deep discount, maybe even below cost.

Usually, inventory is valued at the cost paid to buy the inventory. But in the case of old inventory, that value wouldn't give good information to the reader of the financial statements. Old inventory is not as valuable and should be valued at less than its historical cost if the goods can be sold only at a price less than cost. When companies measure the value of the inventory they hold, accounting rules require the companies to compare the actual cost paid with the market value. The value on the balance sheet is whichever amount is lower.

Net Realizable Value

Another method of asset valuation is usually associated with the receivables on the balance sheet. Accounts receivable are the amounts that customers owe the business. The receivables are increased every time a credit sale is made and decreased every time a customer actually pays the cash for those debts. One of the problems, though, is that not all customers pay, and the business will have some bad debts. Accounts receivable are valued at the net realizable value. Net realizable value is the dollar amount the company actually expects to collect from the receivables. Often, the account title for receivables includes the word *net* after it. Including *net* in the account title signals that the amount on the balance sheet is the result of reducing the total amount of receivables by some estimate of the amount of bad debts.

Historical cost is used as the basis for many asset valuations and is the starting-point value for assets like buildings, equipment, vehicles, and patents. For most tangible and intangible assets, the historical cost is then allocated to expense over the time the asset is used in the business. That expense for tangible assets is depreciation and for intangibles is amortization. Each time some of that cost is expensed, the balance sheet value of the asset is reduced. That reduction in value can be shown in two ways. The first way identifies the account as a *net* amount. On the balance sheet you will often see asset accounts labeled "xxxxxxx, net," where the "xxxxxxx" might be "property, plant, and equipment" or "intangible assets," which means that the account is valued at the historical cost of those assets less the portion of the cost that has already been allocated to expense. The second way to show the reduction of value is to list the historical cost on one line and then include a separate line immediately following that indicates the amount of reduction, called *accumulated depreciation*. Intangible assets rarely use the two-line presentation.

Some assets are not subject to depreciation or amortization. Land and goodwill are two examples. The value of land on the balance sheet remains at cost unless something really unusual happens to reduce the value. Goodwill, an intangible asset that occurs in an acquisition, is not amortized, but the company must do complicated impairment testing to determine whether the goodwill is worth the dollar amount listed on the balance sheet. If it isn't, then the company must reduce the value of the goodwill.

Most assets are currently valued at historical cost, but there are some exceptions for market values. In September 2006, the FASB issued guidance on how to measure market value but didn't expand the use of that measurement. The FASB is doing research on expanding the use of market values for measuring the assets on the balance sheet. In the future, companies may use market values for more assets if the FASB requires it.

Liability Valuation Methods

While asset valuation involves several different methods that are mainly variations of historical cost or market value, liability valuation is limited to two basic methods. Accounting rules dictate that companies measure current liabilities at the *sum of the cash payments necessary to settle the obligation*. Current liabilities are those obligations that are due within one year, and those debts are the first category of liabilities listed on the balance sheet. Examples are taxes, accounts payable, and deferred revenue. This measure tells users of the financial statement how much cash or other assets the company will use to satisfy existing short-term obligations.

The other method of valuing liabilities uses *present-value techniques* and is applied to liabilities that are due sometime beyond the next year. Accounting rules require that companies measure noncurrent liabilities at the present value of the cash payments necessary to settle the debt. To do the calculations requires a discount rate, and for most debts, the interest rate charged by the lender is the discount rate. Some obligations don't have a lender-determined interest rate, and then the company must estimate one. The interest rate choice can have considerable effect on the final balance sheet value. A higher interest rate results in a lower present value, and most companies prefer a lower rather than a higher value for their noncurrent liabilities.

Let's assume a company owes a lender $1,000,000 in five years to settle a debt. The company needs to value that liability on the balance sheet at the present value of $1,000,000. Assuming the lender has not stated an interest rate, the company will determine its own. If the company chooses 5 percent as the rate, the present value of the $1,000,000 is $783,500, whereas the present value using 10 percent is $620,900. Obviously, the company would prefer to use the higher rate to value the debt to show a lower liability on the balance sheet.

Noncurrent liabilities are the second category of liabilities on the balance sheet and include items such as any long-term debt, deferred income taxes, and retirement or pension obligations. Most of the noncurrent liabilities represent debt obligations, but deferred taxes are a little different.

Deferred tax liabilities represent an estimate of taxes that the company will pay in future years because it has taken tax deductions for some items before those items are expenses. This situation happens because the rules governing expenses are very different from the rules that apply to business tax returns. The important thing to understand is that deferred tax liabilities are an estimate of future taxes that the company may pay. Oftentimes, though, the company can engage in activities that legitimately allow it to avoid the payment. The accounting rules for deferred taxes are complicated and are meant to give financial statement users information on possible future tax payments.

Why Is It Important?

Analysts and sophisticated investors use techniques to investigate a company's performance beyond the amount of net income. Those techniques often involve using numbers from the balance sheet to construct ratios. The analyst or investor compares those ratios to industry averages or the ratios of other companies to decide how the performance of one company compares to that of others. Calculating ratios over time also gives investors insight into trends in performance. Some of the most common ratios used in investment analysis are listed in Table 6.1.

Different methods exist for measuring both assets and liabilities, depending on the nature of the thing being measured. Understanding the measurement techniques helps you better scrutinize your portfolio through ratio analysis.

Table 6.1

Name	Formula	Importance/Purpose
Liquidity Ratios		
Current ratio	Current assets/current liabilities	Number of times current assets could cover current liabilities, debt-paying ability
Quick ratio	Current assets − inventory/current liabilities	More stringent test of debt-paying ability due to removal of inventory
Accounts receivable turnover	Net credit sales/average accounts receivable	How many times accounts receivable are collected during the year
Number of days sales in receivables	Number of days in the period/accounts receivable turnover	Number of days the average receivable is outstanding
Inventory turnover	Cost of goods sold/inventory	Measures the efficiency of managing and selling inventory; how many times the inventory turns over
Number of days sale in inventory	Number of days in the period/inventory turnover	The average length of time it takes inventory to turn over
Solvency Ratios		
Debt to equity	Total liabilities/total stockholders' equity	How much of the company's financing is debt
Times interest earned	Net income + interest expense + income tax expense/interest expense	Ability of the company to make the current year's interest payments
Profitability Ratios		
Return on assets	Net income + interest expense, net of tax/average total assets	How much profit the company generated for each $1 of assets; measures returns to the owners and creditors
Return on equity	Income/average owners' equity	Similar to return on assets but measures the return to owners/shareholders
Return on sales	Net income + interest expense, net of tax/net sales	How much profit the company generated for each $1 in sales
Gross profit ratio	Gross profit/net sales	How much gross profit the company generated for each $1 in sales
Earnings per share	Net income/average number of shares of common stock outstanding	Measures the net income on a per-share basis

CHAPTER 7

CASH VERSUS ACCRUAL

Cash basis accounting is easy to understand because that's the method most of us use in our personal life. Accrual accounting, however, follows the rules of revenue recognition and cost allocation. Although research has shown that accrual accounting is a better predictor of future performance, investors still need cash flow information to detect tricks that managers might use to manipulate accrual accounting performance results.

QUICK POINTS: CASH VERSUS ACCRUAL

- ❖ A company using cash basis accounting measures revenue at the amount of cash received from customers and measures expenses at the amount of cash payments.
- ❖ A company using accrual accounting recognizes revenue in the period in which it is earned, *not* when the customer pays.
- ❖ A company using accrual accounting recognizes all the expenses that were necessary to produce the period's revenue, even if no cash was paid for some of those expenses.
- ❖ Accrual basis accounting gives readers of financial statements better information about the performance of a company.
- ❖ Cash flow information is available in the Statement of Cash Flows.
- ❖ You can use information from the Statement of Cash Flows to evaluate and predict investment performance.

Cash Basis Accounting?

Cash basis accounting is the method most of us use for our personal finances. Revenue is any cash inflow. For individuals, those cash inflows are paychecks and perhaps other income such as dividend checks from investments. For companies, those cash flows are the payments from customers. Cash basis expenses are any cash outflow. To measure income on the cash basis, you only look at the change in the checkbook balance during the accounting period.

Accrual Basis Accounting

Accrual accounting ignores the actual cash flow for most revenues and expenses. Revenue for the month (or quarter or year) is all the revenue that meets the criteria to be earned. Expenses for the time period are all those costs that were necessary to generate the revenue the company is recognizing on the period's income statement.

One of the biggest differences between cash basis and accrual basis accounting involves accounting for noncurrent assets. A company using cash basis accounting would not have any depreciation expense. In fact, they wouldn't have any assets except cash. The cost of a building would result in an expense equal to the cost in the year of the purchase. Imagine the effect of building expense of $2,000,000 all on one year's income statement.

How Does Accrual Basis Accounting Give Better Information?

To see the difference between the cash basis and the accrual basis of accounting, we'll look at a small lawn service company that is just starting out in business. During one of the first months of operations, the company mows the lawns of 20 clients, for a total of $2,000. Each client has 30 days to pay the invoice. During that same month, the lawn service buys gasoline for $200 cash and pays the employees $1,000 cash. Using the cash basis of accounting, the total revenues for the month would be $0, since there were no cash receipts, and the total expenses for the month would be $1,200. This would give the company a net loss of $1,200 for the month. Under the accrual basis of accounting, the company would show $2,000 in revenue and $1,200 in expenses, giving it a net income of $800. The accrual basis gives readers of the financial statements a truer picture of the operations and performance of the lawn service company than the cash basis does.

What Cash Flow Information Is Available in the Financial Reports?

The Statement of Cash Flows presents cash basis information to financial statement readers. The Statement of Cash Flows is particularly useful for assessing what the company will do in the future.

The Statement of Cash Flows categorizes cash flows as one of three types. Cash flows are related to operating activities, financing activities, or investing activities. The first section of the Statement of Cash Flows presents information about cash flows from operating activities. The Cash Flows from Operating Activities section explains why net income is different from the change in the amount of cash in the cash account on the balance sheet. This section shows the particulars of cash received and paid for the normal business activities. The Cash Flows from Operating Activities section may be shown using either the direct or the indirect method. Figures 7.1 and 7.2 show the two methods for a fictitious company. Notice that the same net cash flow from operating activities is the result from either method.

The format of the Statement of Cash Flows requires listing the operating section first, but the remaining two sections can be listed in any order. One of those two remaining sections, Cash Flows from Financing Activities, shows the cash received or paid for borrowing and repayments. The cash proceeds from the sale

Figure 7.1   Statement of Cash Flows—Indirect Method.

KAMKEM, Inc. Statement of Cash Flows For the Year Ended December 31, 2007	
Cash Flows from Operating Activities	
Net income	$100,000
Adjustments to reconcile net income to net cash flow	
Depreciation expense	25,000
Increase in accounts receivable	(2,500)
Increase in accounts payable	3,000
Net cash inflow from operating activities	$125,500

of company stock, or repurchases of that stock, and cash dividend payments are also displayed in the financing section. The cash flows from financing activities usually involve liability accounts or stockholders' equity accounts from the balance sheet. This section tells you the amount of cash used or received from financing activities, including financing from investors. Figure 7.3 shows an example of a complete Statement of Cash Flows including Cash Flows from Financing Activities.

Cash Flows from Investing Activities is the last section on the Statement of Cash Flows and reveals the cash paid for noncur-

Figure 7.2   Statement of Cash Flows—Direct Method.

KAMKEM, Inc. Statement of Cash Flows For the Year Ended December 31, 2007	
Cash Flows from Operating Activities	
Cash collected from customers	$170,000
Cash collected from interest	5,500
Cash payments to suppliers	(50,000)
Net cash inflow from operating activities	$125,500

Figure 7.3

KAMKEM, Inc. Statement of Cash Flows For the Year Ended December 31, 2007	
Cash Flows from Operating Activities	
Net income	$100,000
Adjustments to reconcile net income to net cash flow	
Depreciation expense	25,000
Increase in accounts receivable	(2,500)
Increase in accounts payable	3,000
Net cash inflow from operating activities	$125,500
Cash Flows from Financing Activities	
Proceeds of debt	10,000
Repayment of debt	(2,000)
Sale of stock	5,000
Cash dividends	(1,000)
Net cash inflow from financing activities	$12,000
Cash Flows from Investing Activities	
Purchase of equipment	(4,000)
Sale of investment	1,000
Net cash outflow from investing activities	$(3,000)
Net increase in cash	$134,500
Cash balance at beginning of the year	$100,000
Cash balance at end of year	$234,500

rent assets or the proceeds from selling them. In addition to the obvious purchase and sale of investments, common cash flows in this section include the cash paid for the purchase of equipment or vehicles. Note, though, that the actual amount of cash paid is displayed on this statement, not the purchase price. So if a company bought a new piece of equipment costing $12,000 and the seller allows payment over two years with a $4,000 down payment, the cash outflow from investing activities is the $4,000 down payment. Any cash payments are listed in the Cash Flows from Investing Activities section. Any interest included in the repayments is included in the Cash Flows from Operating Activities section. Figure 7.3 shows the complete statement including the cash flows from operating activities.

The Cash Flows from Operating Activities section provides key information about why net income, the accrual measure of company performance, is different from the increase in cash shown on the balance sheet. Remember that revenue is recognized when earned—generally, when the company ships the goods or performs the services involved in the sale. To increase income, the accrual measure, a company could decide to loosen credit requirements and sell to customers with a poorer credit rating. That would increase sales revenue because recognition occurs when goods are shipped not when cash is collected. Selling to riskier customers will increase sales on the income statement but will not increase cash from operating activities on the Statement of Cash Flows because many of those customers will not pay.

Statement of Cash Flows and Investment Analysis

Using the Statement of Cash Flows to examine investments involves looking at the bottom line, the net change in cash for the period, and at the different sections of the statement. The bottom line tells you whether the cash position of the company increased or decreased during the period. But that information is already available by comparing last period's and this period's balance sheets. The change in the amount of cash listed on the balance sheets must be equal to the net change in the amount of cash on the Statement of Cash Flows. Analysis beyond the bottom line helps investors predict dividend and bill-paying ability.

Compare Net Income to Cash Flow

One useful bit of analysis is comparing net income from the income statement to cash flows from operating activities. In companies with large amounts of fixed assets, you would expect net income to be less than cash from operating activities because some expenses that are included in net income are noncash expenses. Depreciation, for example, is an expense that does reduce net income but does not use cash. For companies with a large amount of equipment, vehicles, and buildings, depreciation is a big expense and reduces net income by a large amount. But it does not affect cash flow, so it doesn't reduce cash flow from operating activities. In that case, cash from operating activities should be larger than net income. Monitoring the change in the difference between a company's net income and cash from operating activities tells investors how effectively the income-generating pursuits are providing cash for paying bills and dividends.

Sources and Uses of Cash Flow

A second useful investigation on the Statement of Cash Flows is into the sources and uses of cash flows. The financing section communicates information about the borrowing activities of the company. If the financing section indicates that cash is provided or the net cash from financing activities is an inflow, that means the company took on debt or sold stock. If, instead, cash is used or the net cash from financing activities is an outflow, then the company repaid more than it borrowed or repurchased some of its own stock for treasury stock. The payment of dividends also is a use of cash that is classified in the financing section of the Statement of Cash Flows.

The investing section discloses the company's cash flows associated with noncurrent assets. If the investing section shows cash provided by investing activities or the net cash from investing activities is an inflow, that means the company sold off assets. Those assets could be actual investments or they could be equipment, property, or vehicles. Although the cash inflow is good, a company can't stay in business if it sells off the assets it needs to continue operations. If, instead of cash being provided by investing activities, the investing activities section shows cash used or

net cash outflows, that indicates that the company bought pro-
ductive assets or made some investments.

Significant Noncash Transactions

A final section of the Statement of Cash Flows can provide clues
to other investing and financing activities. This section doesn't
deal with cash at all; it is called Significant Noncash Transactions
and is similar to a footnote or schedule of transactions. In this
section, which is not in the body of the statement but at the end,
a company would disclose actions such as the purchase of an asset
using debt or a seller-financed sale. Only the cash down payment
is reflected in the financing or investing section in the body of
the statement. The noncash portion of the transaction appears in
the Significant Noncash Transactions section at the end of the
Statement of Cash Flows.

PART III

DETECTING THE TRUTH ON THE INCOME STATEMENT AND STATEMENT OF STOCKHOLDERS' EQUITY

CHAPTER 8

REVENUE HOAXES

PROBABLY THE MOST common form of financial statement deception, if not actual fraudulent accounting, involves revenue recognition. Managers manipulate the amount of revenue to achieve the desired target revenue or earnings during a certain time

---

QUICK POINTS: REVENUE HOAXES

- ❖ Timing adjustment of revenue recognition can be done in these two ways:
  - ❖ Revenue recognized too early, which gives the impression of a turn-around or maintenance of strong earnings.
  - ❖ Revenue recognized too late.
- ❖ Fabrication of revenue increases earnings and can be done in these ways:
  - ❖ Round-tripping.
  - ❖ Items shipped but not ordered.
  - ❖ Items shipped to a warehouse and held for future sale.
  - ❖ Nonsales transactions recorded as revenue.
- ❖ The revenue measurement method can present deceptive levels in these ways:
  - ❖ Using gross versus net amounts.
  - ❖ Using side agreements.
- ❖ These tricky revenue recognition situations require judgment:
  - ❖ Multiple revenue streams in one sale, such as a product and service.
  - ❖ Related parties.
  - ❖ Right of return.
- ❖ Detection techniques include:
  - ❖ Ratios.
  - ❖ Notes to the financial statements.

---

period. These revenue hoaxes are accomplished by adjusting the time period in which the revenue is recognized, inventing non-existent sales to boost revenue, and measuring existing revenue in ways that provide the desired effect. Admittedly, some revenue recognition issues are complicated, but the accounting method choice can inflate or depress revenue, depending on how aggressive management wants to be. Through careful inspection of relationships between items on the financial statements, astute readers can find evidence of revenue hoaxes.

Hoax #1: Recognizing Revenue Early

One of the easiest ways to increase revenue is to recognize it early. A legitimate way to recognize revenue sooner rather than later is to simply change the accounting policy. Companies choose the method of revenue recognition they plan to use and disclose that method in the notes to the financial statements. Companies are allowed to change to a more aggressive, earlier recognition of revenue. The only requirement is to include that information in the notes so that careful readers of the financial statements know that a change has occurred. This means that a company that realizes it might not make the target earnings number can change to another method of revenue recognition that will recognize enough revenue to meet the target.

For example, if a company sells a five-year license, it may have the choice of recognizing the revenue over the five years or immediately in the year of the sale, depending on the structure of the transaction. If the company changes from the slower method of recognizing the revenue over the duration of the license to recognizing most of the revenue at the beginning of the license, it has clearly started recognizing revenue earlier and should receive a one-time enhancement to revenue from license sales. The revenue will show up in the income statement now rather than in the future. That could be just enough revenue to meet the forecast or achieve the bonus threshold.

Percentage of Completion

Another example of a policy change that speeds up the recognition of revenue is the situation in which a company that produces a product that takes a long time to complete changes from recognizing revenue at the completion of the product to a method called *percentage of completion*. The percentage-of-completion method recognizes revenue during the production cycle. Construction projects or aerospace products that take several years to complete often use this type of revenue recognition. The change from completed construction to percentage of completion would provide revenue to earlier periods, but it is based on several estimates. Particularly aggressive estimates can overstate the amount of revenue in earlier periods of production. The total amount of revenue is not any different, but the timing is, with some being recognized in earlier accounting periods. When the product is complete, later periods could be left with little revenue remaining. If such a change in method occurs, the company must disclose it in the notes to the financial statements.

Channel Stuffing

Channel stuffing is another way to increase revenue, and it may or may not be illegal, depending on the circumstances. Near the end of the month, quarter, or year, a company entices customers to buy more product than they actually need, promising big discounts and generous return policies. This type of promotion can have a legitimate business purpose beyond artificially increasing revenue because it means the customers will not be buying those products from a competitor. But it can also result in a buildup of customers' inventory, resulting in fewer sales in the next period. Channel stuffing can cross the line into fraudulent accounting when the discounted sales are accompanied by side agreements that guarantee the right of return. If such side agreements exist, the mechanism is little more than temporarily parking inventory at the customers' locations, under the guise of sales. When the customers return that inventory, the large sales returns wipe out the revenue recognized previously.

Bill-and-Hold Sales

Like channel stuffing, recognizing the revenue from bill-and-hold sales may or may not be legitimate. A bill-and-hold sale involves recording revenue before the product is shipped to the customer. Here is how this works. The customer agrees to purchase product but does not have room to store it. Instead, the shipment is sent to another location, where it is held until later delivery to the customer. If the transaction meets certain criteria, which include a written order for the goods with the customer requesting delayed shipment at a future fixed delivery date, then the seller can include the revenue in the current period, even before the items are shipped. Although not always illegal, bill-and-hold sales can result in early revenue recognition and can signal aggressive accounting methods.

Hoax #2: Delaying Revenue Recognition

Although most techniques seek to recognize revenue earlier, some companies benefit by recognizing revenue later. More conservative policies will recognize less revenue in current periods, which could be useful to a company trying to avoid political costs. Oil companies would benefit by not showing very high revenues in order to evade special taxes imposed by Congress. Companies involved in monopoly lawsuits would also want to appear less successful and would choose a revenue recognition method that would put off recognition until future periods, after the lawsuit is settled.

Hoax #3: Fraudulent Revenue Recognition

While companies can justify a change in accounting policy to recognize revenue earlier or legitimately use channel stuffing and bill-and-hold sales to accomplish early revenue recognition, other techniques are fraudulent. This means the revenue is included in income before it is actually earned or before payment, or the likelihood of receiving payment, exists. Accounting rules require companies to include only revenue made during a specific time period on the financial statements reporting on that time period.

Backdating Documents

One trick to increase revenue is to include sales made after the close of the period through backdating documents. This procedure moves next period's sales into the current period, helping to reach the revenue target. The problem, however, is that next period's revenue will probably be short because of the shift to the previous period. Managers who use this technique believe the shortfall is temporary and it will be easy to catch up next period because of better economic conditions, new products, or something else that will make it all right. It doesn't always work that way, though.

Inventing Revenue

At least when adjusting the timing of revenue recognition, companies are recognizing actual sales revenue—just not in the right time period. Another way to increase revenue is to simply make it up. These methods can involve false sales or reclassifying other inflows as revenue.

Round-Tripping

Round-tripping, originally a legitimate barter system for two companies to exchange similar assets without any exchange of cash, has evolved into a revenue fabrication scheme. Two companies agree to exchange similar assets and agree on a price—usually an inflated price—to increase both parties' revenue numbers. The profit is not affected, but the revenue looks much better. That revenue is illusory and is unlikely to be repeated, unless another swap is negotiated. The SEC prohibits round-tripping in some industries, and swaps are considered suspicious in publicly traded companies.

Product Shipment Schemes

Companies can also falsify revenue through product shipment schemes. In some cases, sellers ship items even if the customer has not placed the order. The seller then records the sales revenue because the product has been shipped. A variation of this technique is to ship the products off-site, perhaps to a warehouse, where the items are held for future sale. Shipping documents support the recording of revenue in the current accounting period, even though no sales order exists.

False Classification of Inflow

False revenues can also take the form of classifying other inflows to the company as revenue. The term *revenue* has a very precise meaning in the business. Revenue must be an inflow to the company from selling products or performing services associated with core business activities. Other inflows can come from things like borrowing, rebates, or selling off assets. Including those nonrevenue inflows with legitimate revenue gives a false picture of future profitability.

Hoax #4: Deceptive Revenue Measurement

Companies can use deceptive methods for measuring the amount of revenue. In some cases, users of financial statements focus not on the amount of profit but, rather, on the amount of revenue. In such situations, companies are motivated to report revenues at the largest possible number. Grossing up revenue is one practice that presents a very large, but unrealistic, revenue number. The seller records the gross amount of revenue when only entitled to a commission on the sale. For example, a consignment shop acts as an agent for the owner of an item. If the shop grossed up revenues, it would record as revenue the entire amount received for the sale of items, even though it must remit all but a small percentage to the owners of the items. Although the cash flow to the owner is recorded, if the focus is on the amount of revenue on the income statement, then the goal of higher revenue is accomplished.

Sales with Side Agreements

Another measurement trick involves making sales with side agreements. The company makes sales to customers with generous return privileges, when those returns will likely take place in a future period. In some cases, the sale involves a side agreement— a secret letter that allows the customer to return the goods. The terms of the side agreement can include the right to return the purchased goods if the customer is unable to sell the goods at a certain price. The deception occurs because the revenue is recorded when the goods are shipped, but that revenue amount is likely to be reversed in a future period when the goods are returned.

Tricky Revenue Recognition Situations

Sometimes the revenue recognition situation is complicated. For example, when a company is involved in the sale of software, there may be other services that are packaged along with that sale. The sale of the software may include services such as technical support and upgrades. When this is the case, the revenue has to be allocated between the actual software and the services. A company can recognize a portion of the revenue from the sale of the software when there has been an order from a customer, the software has been delivered, the price is fixed, and it is probable the receivable will be collected. The remaining portion of the revenue can be recognized over the life of the license or service agreement.

Detection Techniques: Check the Trends and Ratios

One way to check on the legitimacy of revenue is to scrutinize the amount of revenue reported. Calculate the rate of change from one quarter to the next to find the trend or pattern to revenues. Further investigate those changes in revenue that are not explained by seasonality. On the balance sheet, the trend in the allowance for bad debts should track the trend in accounts receivable. Big changes in that amount without a similar change in accounts receivable should be a red flag to the reader of the financial report. A third trend to follow is the difference between net income and cash from operating activities. If cash from operating activities begins to significantly lag behind net income, it could be a sign that the company is engaging in some revenue hoaxes.

In addition to the trend of revenue over time, it is useful to compare a company's change in revenue with those of other companies in the same industry through industry averages, available from subscription services. If you live near a public college or university, the library may allow community members to use its subscription for a small fee. Changes that are very different from those reported by other companies in the same business warrant further investigation.

In addition to considering the revenue changes, you can also detect revenue hoaxes through ratios involving accounts receivable. As you remember from Chapter 4, a company can include the revenue in income before the cash is collected, as long as the transaction meets the criteria for being earned. If accounts receivable increase, that indicates the revenue is recognized but not collected. The balance sheet amount of accounts receivable that increases at a faster rate than the rate of increase in revenue is a sign that customers are taking longer to pay. A legitimate reason for this situation is the existence of a difficult economic environment for customers who are part of one particular industry.

For example, if Company A's customers are mainly home builders, Company A's accounts receivable may increase faster than revenue if the housing market slows suddenly. The home builders will have trouble paying their bills and will take longer to pay Company A for past purchases. However, in this situation, the customers (home builders) would probably not continue to make purchases, so Company A would see a decrease in revenue, too.

An increase in accounts receivable without an accompanying increase in revenue could also be a warning sign of bogus sales or premature recognition of revenue. If the company fabricated the sales, there are no customers who will be paying. If the revenue is from real sales that were recognized early, it will simply take longer for customers to pay.

Another sign of trouble is a change in certain ratios involving accounts receivable. Three ratios in particular can provide clues to the analyst. The first analytic is a change in the accounts receivable turnover. (See Chapter 6.) A decrease in the turnover ratio over time or a turnover ratio lower than the industry average means the company is not receiving payment quickly enough. The reason could be tough economic times hitting customers who are mainly in one industry. A decreasing receivables turnover ratio could also indicate boosting revenue by selling to customers with poor credit.

The second ratio tool useful for investigating revenue hoaxes is the ratio measuring number of days to collect accounts receivable. (See Chapter 6.) Obviously, if this ratio increases, customers are taking longer to pay. It may be that customers aren't paying because of a revenue hoax.

The third ratio tool is checking the percentage of assets represented by accounts receivable. An increasing percentage suggests a structural change in the company. Normally you'd expect an increase in receivables to be consistent with changes in inventories and other assets used in the business. The logic is that more receivables are the result of higher sales, and higher sales are sustained by more inventory, equipment, and other business assets. If all the assets aren't increasing, then accounts receivable's percentage of assets will increase and that could be a clue to the recognition of false revenue.

Detection Techniques: Check the Notes at the End of Financial Statements

The first place in the notes to check for revenue hoaxes is the first note summarizing the significant accounting policies. In that note you will find information on the revenue recognition method. The Procter & Gamble 2006 annual report presents two paragraphs describing the revenue recognition methods used by the company. Compare that to the IBM 2004 annual report that uses three paragraphs just to state the general policy for revenue recognition and then goes into detail for each major revenue category plus special situations. It's a good idea to compare last year's revenue recognition note to this year's to spot any unusual changes that might not be reflected in other note disclosures.

The notes to the financial statements also disclose changes in accounting principle. For some transactions, there is more than one correct way to measure or report the event. For example, construction companies can recognize revenue by the percentage-of-completion method or the completed contract method. Retail sellers can recognize revenue in the normal manner, at the time the product is delivered, or they can use the installment method or the cost recovery method. All of these methods of recognizing revenue are acceptable. If the company consistently uses the same method, investors can easily compare performance from one period to the next.

Companies can change the application of accounting principle from one correct method to another correct method, but they must disclose that change in the notes. This disclosure alerts readers to a possible lack of comparability from one period to the next. This is particularly important for spotting revenue hoaxes. Changing from the completed contract method to percentage of completion represents a move to recognize revenue earlier than in the past. Carefully investigate changes in revenue recognition policies to find clues to deceptive reporting. Another change that should alert readers is a change to a later period end date. This allows the company to include a few more days' sales in the quarterly earnings. However, such a change must be disclosed in the notes to the financial reports.

CHAPTER 9

EXPENSE DODGES

ACCOUNTING RULES DICTATE that companies should include on the income statement all the expenses necessary to generate the revenues that are recognized on that income statement. But company management may need to "adjust" the expenses to meet forecast earnings, bonus thresholds, or other target income numbers. That adjustment can involve actions to postpone, reduce, or completely eliminate the recognition of the expenses, thereby artificially increasing income in the current accounting period. The trouble with postponement, though, is that eventually those expenses will have to be included on a future income statement, reducing the income of a period that has its own legitimate expenses. Continual delay in recognizing expenses causes a backlog, and the dollar amount grows. Eventually that huge amount of delayed expense will have to show up on a future income statement.

QUICK POINTS: EXPENSE DODGES

✧ Company management can postpone expenses by recording them as assets.
✧ Managers can reduce expenses in any one accounting period by using favorable estimates.
✧ Managers can use reserves to offset expenses.
✧ Before 2005, some expenses would never appear on the income statement if management made a change in accounting principle.

Other adjustment techniques reduce the amount of the expense in the current period by changing estimates to stretch out the amount of expense over several time periods, thereby reducing the amount in any one period. Managers can also reduce expenses by using reserve amounts to offset the legitimate expenses of the period. Another adjustment technique avoids the expense buildup problem by bypassing the income statement completely. A change in accounting policies can provide the perfect solution by doing just that.

The effect of these adjustments is to dodge the rules that require certain expenses to be on the income statement in a certain time period. By avoiding the proper recognition of expenses, the income statement doesn't give a true picture of the performance of the company. Fortunately, the financial statements offer clues that alert readers can find. Identification of the clues will help readers find these expense dodges.

Dodge #1: Capitalize Rather Than Record an Expense for Cash Payments

One easy, and sometimes legitimate, way to dodge an expense is to record the payment as an asset instead. This method is applied correctly for most items that are used over several years by the business. The cost of the item is recorded as an asset, and then a portion of that cost is expensed during each accounting period that the asset is used. This is common and correct for buildings, equipment, vehicles, and other assets used in operations. Capitalizing, or recording a cost as an asset, and the subsequent expensing are proper and represent good matching of the expense of the asset with the revenues generated by the use of it.

This correct method, however, can be perverted, and companies can improperly capitalize costs. One area of business susceptible to improper capitalization is that of postacquisition expenditures associated with assets. Costs of repairing and maintaining buildings, for example, may be an immediate expense or may be capitalized, depending on the nature of the expenditure.

The accounting rules identify different types of repair and maintenance costs. Ordinary repairs and maintenance just preserve the operating condition of the asset and are expensed, and should be expensed, immediately. Additions and improvements change the asset and are capitalized and the cost expensed through depreciation in future periods. The company management must use judgment to classify the expenditure as either an expense or a capital expenditure. For example, if new flooring is installed in a building, management must determine whether that flooring is simply a repair that keeps the building in working order or if it changes the building in a way that increases efficiency or useful life. Good management will establish a policy that reduces the amount of judgment involved, capitalizing expenditures that will provide a future benefit and expensing all others.

In some cases, capitalization of expenses signals a company that is aggressively attempting to move expenses out of the current period. One example is the capitalization of the costs of new financing, whether it is a new public offering of stock or issuance of bonds. In both cases, legal and accounting expertise is needed to accomplish the financing, and both involve large printing costs. Theoretically, these costs do benefit the company over future periods and so would qualify for capitalization. Most companies, however, expense these costs. So when a company does capitalize the costs of new financing, you can take it as a sign that it is aggressively looking to postpone expenses. Another example is the costs of opening new stores. A company could argue that the preopening costs really benefit time periods when the new store is open and therefore can legitimately be capitalized. If a company does capitalize the preopening costs, it is wise to investigate the amortization period for those costs. A long time period—more than about two years—reveals an expense dodge.

Several specific types of expenditures require so much judgment in determining the proper treatment—either to capitalize or to expense—that we'll take a look at them individually. Costs associated with software and marketing also provide companies with opportunities to dodge expenses. Companies can capitalize software costs if the stage of development has certain characteristics. Once the program is technologically feasible, the company can capitalize, rather than expense, the costs associated with the software. But determining technological feasibility is very subjective and provides a great opportunity for management to dodge an expense.

In most instances, companies expense marketing and advertising costs. But there is an exception that allows capitalization of costs for direct-response advertising with certain characteristics. Namely, the ads must target customers who have responded to such ads in the past. Management determines whether the direct-response advertising campaign qualifies for capitalization based on criteria, but the criteria are subjective and the determination requires management judgment. That subjectivity provides an opportunity for management to dodge an expense by deciding that the direct-response advertising is eligible for capitalization. AOL used this method and capitalized the costs associated with all the software disks it distributed for free in the 1990s. In 1996, however, it wrote off those capitalized costs because the SEC disagreed with management's judgment on capitalizing them.

Like software costs and advertising costs, the costs associated with research and development, which usually have a future use, are generally expensed. But again like software costs and advertising costs, some research and development costs can be capitalized if the costs are for something that has a use other than for the research and development of a specific project. Determining the existence of that future use, however, requires management interpretation and judgment. This provides one more opportunity to dodge an expense through capitalization of costs. Because the conclusions regarding future use are so subjective, capitalization of research and development costs is unusual.

Finally, a legitimate way of putting off an expense through capitalization is the capitalization of interest on self-constructed assets. For example, if a company is constructing a building for its own use, it can capitalize the interest on the construction loan during the time of construction. The logic is that if the company hired a contractor to do the construction, the contract price charged by the contractor would be the cost of the construction loan. It seems fair that a company acting as its own contractor should be able to include interest as a capitalized cost.

Companies can postpone expenses by capitalizing the costs. When they capitalize costs, the company will allocate those costs to future accounting periods, thereby avoiding an expense that reduces income in the current period. The opportunities to engage in this dodge arise because of the judgment involved in determining whether the costs are expenses or are eligible for capitalization. It is that subjectivity that allows companies to dodge expenses.

Dodge #2: Use the Most Favorable Estimates

The theoretical rule is to allocate the cost over the useful life of the asset, accomplishing the matching of the cost with the revenue generated by the asset. Although for tax purposes asset classes have specified lives, for financial reporting no such classification exists. In many situations, management must estimate the time over which to depreciate or amortize the costs associated with an asset. This provides an opportunity for expense dodge #2, using the most favorable estimates.

Management also uses estimates in a special case associated with asset value—that of impairment. An asset's value is impaired if the expected net cash flows from using the asset are less than the carrying value of the asset. The carrying value is the cost less depreciation taken to date. The amount of the impairment loss is equal to the excess of the carrying value over the market value of the asset. To apply the impairment rule, management must estimate future net cash flows. This includes the revenues generated by the asset, any cash received or paid at the time of disposal, and any other cash flows associated with the asset between the date of analysis and the date of disposal. Then the net cash flows are compared to the market value of the asset, which may be part estimate. Obviously, most of these numbers are not precise, and managers may be motivated to use estimates that result in the desired effect.

Dodge #3: Make Use of Reserves

Reserves allow management to control when the expense is on the income statement. Some expenses require estimates to accomplish matching. Items like bad debt expense and warranties are good examples. If a company sells a product with a warranty, the revenue from the sale of the product is recognized when the product is delivered and payment is likely. The matching principle requires that all the expenses associated with generating that revenue be included on the income statement that recognizes the revenue. This means that the cost of the warranty must be included in the same income statement as the sales revenue from the product. The problem is that those warranty costs usually happen in a later period.

Because the precise cost of the warranty is unknown in the current accounting period, management analyzes historical patterns and estimates the warranty expense. While the estimated expense is included on the income statement, the amount of the estimate is also shown as a liability for warranty work on the balance sheet. Then, when the actual warranty costs become known, the company performs the warranty work and reduces the estimated liability by the actual amount of warranty cost. If the estimates prove to be too small, then the company must catch up and take a bigger expense in one period. Likewise, if the estimates prove to be too large, then the company reduces the liability and includes an item on the income statement that actually increases income by reducing the negative amount of the expense.

This methodology allows managers to take large estimated expenses in good years and then release them in bad years, resulting in a smoother income trend. This technique became so widespread that in a speech in 1998 at the New York University Center for Law and Business, Arthur Levitt, former chairman of the SEC, identified it as one of five accounting tricks. Other expenses susceptible to using reserves to dodge expenses include bad debt expense, sales returns, restructuring charges, and loan losses. In each of these cases, management must estimate the expense before the actual amount is known. If it's a good year, managers are motivated to set up a generous reserve because the current period's income can withstand the expense, and then when a future year's income needs a little help, the manager can use the overestimate in the reserve to increase income in the future period.

The use of dodge #3 is not as prevalent as in the past. Currently, the SEC watches for release of reserve amounts, and such an action brings closer scrutiny of the company's financial reports.

Dodge #4: Change the Rules and Skip the Income Statement

Dodges #1 and #2, both ways of postponing expenses, still result in a problem for the company because eventually the expenses will be included on an income statement. Sometimes the postponement causes an even larger expense amount sometime in the future. To avoid this problem, management could decide to change from one correct to another correct method of accounting for that expense and avoid the income statement completely. A new accounting rule in 2005 eliminated this way to dodge expenses.

Detection Techniques: Check the Trends and Ratios

Trends and ratios can detect expense dodges. To detect excessive capitalized costs, compare the increase in capitalized costs over a period of time to the increase in revenue over that same period. You would expect the two rates of increase to be similar. If capitalized costs are increasing at a faster rate than revenue, it is a sign that the company is using dodge #1.

Ratios can also be useful in finding clues to favorable estimates, or dodge #2. Although the accounting policy note presents the depreciable lives the company uses for depreciation, sometimes that information is not detailed enough. In situations that give a wide range for the useful life, you can calculate the average useful life of the assets. Begin by calculating the cost of average depreciable assets for the year. The depreciable assets exclude land and assets under construction, and the details of the values are usually in the annual report. Find the depreciable assets for two consecutive years and divide by 2 to get the average depreciable assets for the year. The next step is to divide the cost of depreciable assets by the annual depreciation expense. The result is a rough approximation of the average useful life.

Using information from the 2005 PepsiCo SEC Form 10-K, shown in Figure 9.1, we can calculate the average useful life of the assets for PepsiCo in 2005. The depreciable assets for 2005 (in millions) are $15,394 ($17,145 − $685 − $1,066), and the depreciable assets for 2004 (in millions) are $14,555 ($15,930 − $646 − $729). To get the average depreciable assets, add those two amounts and divide by 2: $15,394 + $14,555 = $29,949/2 = $14,974.50. The next step is to divide $14,974.50 by the depreciation expense of $1,103, and the result is the average useful life of 13.58 years. If you look at the composition of PepsiCo's depreciable assets for 2005, 76 percent of them are machinery and equipment. The average useful life of about 14 years appears appropriate for that mix.

Analyzing the trend of expenses is one way to discover whether a company is dodging expenses by using reserves. The rate of change in expenses should be the same as the rate of change in revenue. If expenses are increasing faster than revenue, it could be a sign that the company is setting up reserves to later offset expenses. In particular, you would expect that the changes in

Figure 9.1.   From PepsiCo Inc. 2005 10-K Note 4 Property Plant and Equipment (in millions)

	12/31/05	12/31/06
Land and improvements	$ 685	$ 646
Buildings and improvements	3,736	3,605
Machinery and equipment, including fleet and software	11,658	10,950
Construction in progress	1,066	729
	17,145	15,930
Accumulated depreciation	(8,464)	(7,781)
	$ 8,681	$ 8,149
Depreciation expense	$ 1,103	$ 1,062

bad debts and warranties would grow at a rate similar to that of revenue.

Detection Techniques: Check the Notes

The first note on accounting policies will contain information on the capitalization policy. Compare the current year's capitalization guidelines to the previous year, looking for changes. Take special note of the policies with regard to individual assets named in the policy. The note should declare a policy for advertising, software, and research and development. Other items may signal aggressive capitalization. For example, a retailer that is capitalizing the cost of its website development suggests that the company is trying to push those costs to future periods. The company could maintain that it is theoretically sound to capitalize website development costs and then, when the website is producing online sales, match the expense through amortization.

In addition to comparing the company's capitalization policy over time, it is also a good idea to compare with policies of competitors or other companies in the same industry. That comparison will provide a benchmark for the normal capitalization policy for an industry. In the example of the company capitalizing website development costs, the policy would not be considered terribly aggressive if similar retailers were using the same method.

Sometimes uncovering deceptive accounting is as simple as critically assessing the statements made in the notes. Question any unusual costs the company capitalizes if the resulting capitalized asset doesn't have a market value. For example, capitalizing commissions on sales of memberships just doesn't make any sense. In addition, investigate special charges that write down previously capitalized assets. Those charges are an indication that the assets weren't worth the capitalized value, suggesting that they never should have been capitalized. Aggressive capitalization in the past should alert you to the possibility of the same problem in the future.

CHAPTER 10

ONE-TIME CHARGES AND OTHER FORMAT FAKES

THIS CHAPTER REQUIRES you to understand the different parts of the income statement and the significance of locating a revenue or an expense in one section of the statement rather than another. To aid in that understanding, we need a quick overview of the income statement, in order to appreciate the importance of the classification of revenues and expenses.

Overview of the Income Statement

The purpose of the income statement is to show a measure of the company's performance during a period of time. The current

---

QUICK POINTS: ONE-TIME CHARGES AND OTHER FORMAT FAKES

❖ Classification of a revenue or expense as an operating item sends the message that it will continue in the future.

❖ Classification of a revenue or expense as a one-time charge, and calling it a gain or loss, gives the impression that the amount won't recur and therefore readers may disregard it.

❖ Companies making acquisitions can use accounting tricks to increase income.

❖ Restructuring charges are another way to pull negative amounts into the section of the income statement that is often ignored by analysts.

❖ Investors can detect format fakes through trend analysis and careful reading of the notes to the financial reports.

---

shareholders or potential investors can use the income statement to evaluate that company's performance relative to itself in the past. The financial statement users will compare the current period's earnings to previous time periods to see whether the company is doing better, doing worse, or holding steady. The users can also compare the performance of two companies to determine which is doing better during the same time period.

The income statement can have one of two formats. The single-step format first identifies all the revenues, then all the expenses, to come up with an income number. The multiple-step format lists sales revenue first and deducts the cost of the goods sold to arrive at gross profit or gross margin. Then the other expenses and revenues are listed, winding up with an income number. The multiple-step format highlights the difference between the selling price and the cost of the inventory sold.

Although the formats are slightly different, some common features exist. Both formats identify a measure of income associated with the normal operations of the company. Oftentimes this is called *operating income* and includes the normal revenues and expenses of the main business activities. Both formats also identify a measure of income before taxes. This measure includes the operating income plus other increases and decreases to income that aren't categorized as operating and excludes items categorized as extraordinary or discontinued operations. Both formats must separate out increases and decreases in earnings that are the result of nonoperating activities, the events not related to the core business activities of the company. The purpose for this division is to help the user of the income statement discern the revenues and expenses that will continue. The items that will continue are used to predict future performance.

For example, imagine you are looking at the income statement of two different companies in the same type of business. Company Orange has net income of $465 million, and Company Green has net income of $468 million. They seem to be performing equally well based on net income. When you inspect the income statement of Company Orange, though, you notice that listed near the end of the income statement is a $37 million extraordinary gain. Company Green has no extraordinary items on its income statement. Company Orange has a one-time item that makes up nearly 8 percent of its income.

To make better comparisons, users of income statements make adjustments to net income. They just ignore the one-time charges and evaluate based on income numbers that don't contain entries such as discontinued operations, restructuring charges, and extraordinary items. In the Company Orange and Company Green example, users would adjust Company Orange's net income to $428 million, removing the extraordinary gain of $37 million from the income. The comparison would then be Company Orange's net income of $428 million to Company Green's net income of $468 million. The problem with that well-known adjustment, though, is that if judgment is involved in the decision to classify an item as a one-time charge versus a regular operating item, companies are motivated to classify things in a way that is most beneficial to them, obscuring the measure of performance. That means classifying losses as one-time charges and gains as operating items.

Format Fake #1: Floating Around on the Income Statement

Something close to a hierarchy of revenue exists. Sales revenue is "better" than other revenue and gains. The quality of the revenue is based on how likely it is to continue. Investors perceive sales revenue as the most desirable revenue because the company can continue to make sales that produce income in future accounting periods. On the other hand, a gain from the sale of an investment can't occur again because that investment can't be sold more than once.

A similar hierarchy of expenses also exists. Cost of goods sold and operating expenses are considered continuing expenses, but items identified with the terms *loss* and *charge* are often disregarded because they are not recurring. In fact, one common income measure used in financial analysis—earnings before interest, taxes, depreciation, and amortization (EBITDA)—ignores most income statement items after operating income. Managers are motivated to hide weak operating results by using format fake #1.

Format Fake #2: The Big Bath

Although it doesn't seem logical, at times managers are motivated to increase the amount of a company's loss. A financial big bath occurs when a net loss is made even larger by discretionary write-offs and charges. Often, the actual size of the loss doesn't matter. Just the existence of a net loss brings punishment in the form of debt covenant violations or decreased stock prices. Managers increase the loss to move future expenses or negative charges from future periods to the current period. On the face of it, the actions seem conservative, but they really inflate earnings in future periods, making the company's performance look better. Gateway took a big bath in 1997. The stock dropped immediately, but then in the next year the stock was up 83 percent.

This technique is especially useful for a newly hired CEO. By taking a big bath in an early period, the new executive can blame the problems on the previous management team. Then, when future periods show improvement because of the shifting of expenses out of those periods, the new CEO can take credit for the success.

Format Fake #3: Acquisition Tricks

Acquisition accounting is full of techniques that can distort earnings. The purchase price paid for the acquisition is allocated to the assets acquired, with any remaining amount attributed to goodwill. The first common trick involves the research and development activities of the acquired company. Companies can write off as a charge the value of research and development projects that are in process at the time of the acquisition that are determined to have no future value. That one-time charge reduces income once for the full amount in the current period.

Valuing the assets purchased requires judgment, and often companies will assign a high value to in-process research and development activities, with much of the value associated with projects that are immediately charged off because of no future value. That allocation reduces the amount of goodwill, which is evaluated regularly and charged off as the value declines. That trick inflates the earnings of future periods by taking a big charge at acquisition instead of in future periods, when the value of goodwill decreases. Another common trick involves reserves for completing the acquisition. Companies make acquisitions without full knowledge of all the problems. They often set up a reserve, with a charge to income, for unforeseen costs of the acquisition. That charge reduces income in the current period and later, when an actual unforeseen problem arises, the reserve is reduced but income is not affected. Again, this trick moves future expenses to the current period and inflates the earnings of those future periods.

Format Fake #4: Restructuring to Hide Expenses

Companies take restructuring charges when closing locations, laying off employees, or eliminating products or services. Restructuring is distinct from discontinued operations, which has its own section of the income statement. The costs associated with restructuring involve judgment and can involve manipulating expenses to the current period, resulting in lower future expenses and higher future income. Restructuring charges involve assets that have lost value and adding that loss to the restructuring charge. The employee costs become severance pay, a one-time charge, rather than salary expense, an ongoing expense until the employees cease working for the company. In addition, companies set up reserves to cover restructuring costs. Reserves reduce net income in the current period for costs that will occur in future periods. When those costs occur, the reserve is reduced but no reduction in income occurs. Kodak has been incurring massive restructuring charges of over $1 billion a year since 2004, as it downsizes its film business and moves into digital products.

Detection Techniques: Ratios

Investors can do some quantitative analysis by tracking the changes in expenses. A good way to do this is to choose a base year and check the percentage increase for subsequent years. You do this by dividing each year's operating expenses by the sales for that year. Then calculate the ratio for the next year and compare. The amount should stay relatively stable. A decrease of more than 2 percent could indicate that the company has shifted a regular expense into a one-time charge.

Statements with clearly identified nonrecurring charges provide the opportunity to track those charges directly. Divide the nonrecurring amount by total sales. If the average over a number of years is more than 3 percent, the company may be shifting regular expenses into the nonrecurring category.

Another analysis technique monitors the change in reserves—usually liabilities on the balance sheet. The reserves are usually listed in the notes to the financial statements. If you have a PDF form of the statement, do a simple "find" search for the word "reserve" to find the location of all disclosures concerning reserves. A large decrease in reserves suggests that the company might have offset expenses with a decrease in reserves.

Any large write-off or one-time charge may be a mechanism to shift future expenses into the current period, thus making the company look more profitable in the future. Write-offs of receivables are particularly suspect because uncollectible receivables could be the result of phony revenue. Large charges for obsolete inventory can also signal manipulation of inventory cost into the current period, causing future income to be artificially high without a realistic cost for the inventory sold. Additionally, write-downs of inventory should be classified as an operating expense, not a one-time charge.

Detection Techniques: Notes

A careful reading of the notes to the financial statements can alert investors to acquisition tricks. The note on accounting policies must include information on consolidation policies and goodwill. Another note must describe the acquisition and divestiture activities that took place during the year. Large charges relating to acquisitions can mean the acquisition wasn't a positive thing for the company. The note disclosure on acquisitions also presents the allocation of the purchase price to the assets and liabilities of the acquired company. Reading through the notes on accounting policies and the information on acquisitions can help investors spot problems in their portfolios.

CHAPTER 11

CRAFTY COMPREHENSIVE INCOME

SOMEWHERE IN THE financial statements—either at the end of the income statement, in a separate income statement, or on the statement of changes in equity—you'll find a section relating to comprehensive income. We usually think of *comprehensive* as meaning all-inclusive, and that is applicable to this section. The key point, though, is that the items included in this section are often the result of incomplete transactions and certainly don't represent sales. A good understanding of comprehensive income is necessary not only to accurately assess past performance but to predict future performance of your investment.

QUICK POINTS: CRAFTY COMPREHENSIVE INCOME

- ✦ The language is confusing: comprehensive income is different from net income and is different from other comprehensive income.
- ✦ Comprehensive income is equal to net income plus other comprehensive income.
- ✦ Other comprehensive income consists of any changes in equity that do not show up on the income statement.
- ✦ Three specific items are currently displayed in other comprehensive income:
    - ✦ Foreign currency translation amounts.
    - ✦ Additional pension liability adjustment.
    - ✦ Unrealized gains and losses from changes in the value of investments.
- ✦ Other comprehensive income also shows up in the equity section of the balance sheet.

- Companies can report other comprehensive income in one of three ways:
  - A separate income statement with information only about other comprehensive income items.
  - As an added section to the existing income statement.
  - As a section in the statement providing information on changes in stockholders' equity.
- Comprehensive income and the components of other comprehensive income inform the reader of:
  - The change in net assets of the company, including certain gains and losses that aren't normally included in income.
  - The effect of some unrealized gains and losses on the value of the company.

What Is Comprehensive Income?

Comprehensive income is the sum of net income and other comprehensive income. The purpose of comprehensive income is to show the change in the value of the company—net assets—from all sources other than investment by owners. Those changes are the result of common transactions like sales and other economic events that affect the value of the company's assets and liabilities. For example, the changing market value of investments held by a company will change the value of the assets of the company. For most investments, though, that change in value is not recognized on the balance sheet or in income until the actual sale of the investment results in a realized gain or loss. Net income doesn't include the unrealized gains and losses, but comprehensive income does.

What Is Other Comprehensive Income?

Comprehensive income is partitioned into two parts: net income and other comprehensive income. The net income part is easy to understand. It consists of the revenues and expenses associated with the operating activities of the company plus the usual gains and losses that are recognized in the reporting period. Net income also includes the results of discontinued operations and extraordinary items. Other comprehensive income is composed of unrecognized gains and losses. Other comprehensive income consists of four categories: foreign currency items, minimum pension liability adjustments, unrealized gains and losses on certain types of investments, and the unrealized gain on a certain type of derivative.

The first category, foreign currency items, relates to companies that are translating financial statements from a foreign currency into U.S. dollars. Because of the way the translation rules operate, an adjustment is needed to get the balance sheet to balance. That amount can be either a gain or a loss and will actually be recognized in net income when the investment in a foreign company is sold. Until that happens, though, the translation adjustment is part of other comprehensive income and represents an unrecognized gain or loss.

The second category of other comprehensive income is minimum pension liability adjustments. A company must record a minimum pension liability if the pension plan is underfunded when measured against the benefits earned by employees at year-end. Most of the time, this situation occurs because of changes to the pension plan that benefit current employees. Sometimes, though, the situation occurs because of structural changes in characteristics of employees, resulting in actuarial losses. This unusual situation results in a negative amount in other comprehensive income and a corresponding contraequity amount in the stockholders' equity section of the balance sheet. A minimum pension liability adjustment in comprehensive income is a warning sign that the pension plan is underfunded and may require more cash contributions from the company.

The third category of other comprehensive income is unrealized gains and losses from changes in the value of certain investments. Changes in value are called *unrealized gains* and *unrealized losses* because the sale of the investments hasn't taken place to lock in the gain or loss. The change in value of most investments is easy to determine, and the accounting rule makers decided to reflect the changes in value of those investments on the balance sheet. However, the rule makers decided not to recognize all unrealized gains and losses in income and instead to recognize only one kind. For most investments, the changes in value show up in other comprehensive income. When those investments are sold and the gain or loss is realized, the unrealized gain or loss is adjusted out of other comprehensive income. Those adjustments are sometimes called *reclassification adjustments.*

The final component of other comprehensive net income is a complicated unrealized gain or loss associated with cash flow hedges. A cash flow hedge is a derivative financial instrument held by a company to offset any changes in value of a future transaction. In effect, the hedge reduces the risk that the cash flows will be different than expected. To be effective, the value of the hedge will move in the opposite direction of the value of the future transaction.

For example, if a U.S. company is going to make a payment of 400,000 euros in two years, the number of dollars it will take to get 400,000 euros will change depending on the exchange rate. To offset the risk of it costing more dollars than anticipated, the company will buy a hedge contract to receive 400,000 euros in two years. As the exchange rate fluctuates, the number of dollars necessary to make the future payment will be the same as the number of dollars that the company can buy with the 400,000 euros it will receive. The accounting rules require the effective unrealized gain or loss on the hedge to be included in other comprehensive income. So if the exchange rate increases the number of dollars it takes to pay 400,000 euros, the value of the hedge will increase by the same amount. That unrealized gain from the increase in value of the hedge will be shown in the other comprehensive income section. In the real world, perfect cash flow hedges rarely exist and the ineffective portion of the hedge is included in net income.

Currently, other comprehensive income has only four components, but that may change. When the accounting rule requiring companies to reveal other comprehensive income was first imposed, only three components were identified. The effective portion of cash flow hedges was added when a new accounting standard relating to hedges took effect. New accounting rules, particularly ones that involve unrealized gains and losses, may add more components to other comprehensive income.

Where in the Financial Reports Do You Find Comprehensive Income?

Accounting rules require companies to show on the face of financial statements net income, other comprehensive income, and comprehensive income. The rules don't specify exactly where, but they suggest several ways to accomplish this. Companies can choose from three alternative ways of presenting comprehensive income. The easiest to understand is a separate financial statement. That statement starts with net income, then lists the four components, if a company has any of those transactions, and then adds the components to net income to disclose comprehensive earnings.

A second way to present comprehensive income is to append other comprehensive income to the end of the income statement. After net income, another section follows that is labeled "other comprehensive income," displaying the required components. The total of other comprehensive income is added to net income to arrive at comprehensive income.

The most difficult-to-understand presentation is to include the components of comprehensive income in the Statement of Stockholders' Equity. In addition to the usual information about changes in the stock accounts and retained earnings, another column is shown for the components of other comprehensive income. The column may be labeled "Other Comprehensive Income," but it often is titled something about unrealized gains and losses not affecting income. The total of all the changes identified on the Statement of Stockholders' Equity is comprehensive income.

Following are two examples of the different presentations of comprehensive income. Figure 11.1 is taken from the 2005 IBM 10-K. This presentation is the most difficult to understand, as

Figure 11.1   Consolidated Statement of Stockholders' Equity

International Business Machines Corporation and Subsidiary Companies				
(Dollars in Millions)				
	Common Stock and Additional Paid-in Capital	*Retained Earnings*	*Treasury Stock*	*Accumulated Gains (and Losses) Not Affecting Earnings*	*Total*
2005					
Stockholders' equity, January 1, 2005	$26,673	$38,148	$(31,072)	$(2,061)	$31,688
Net income plus gains and (losses) not affecting retained earnings:					
Net income		7,934			$7,934
Gains and (losses) not affecting retained earnings (net of tax):					
Net unrealized gains on SFAS No. 133 cash flow hedge derivatives (net of tax expense of $502)				891	891
Foreign currency translation adjustments (net of tax expense of $345)				(1,153)	(1,153)
Minimum pension liability adjustment (net of tax expense of $320)				290	290
Net unrealized gains on marketable securities (net of tax expense of $8)				17	17

Total gains and (losses) not affecting retained earnings				45
Subtotal: Net income plus gains and (losses) not affecting retained earnings				$7,979
Cash dividends declared— common stock		(1,250)		(1,250)
Common stock issued under employee plans (18,572,017 shares)	2,257			2,257
Purchases (606,697 shares) and sales (2,594,786 shares) of treasury stock under employee plans—net		(98)	197	99
Other treasury shares purchased, not retired (90,237,800 shares)			(7,671)	(7,671)
Decrease in shares remaining to be issued in acquisition	(24)			(24)
Income tax benefits—stock transactions	20			20
Stockholders' equity, December 31, 2005	$28,926	$44,734	$(38,546)	$(2,016)	$33,098

was just discussed. The column is titled "Accumulated Gains (and Losses) Not Affecting Retained Earnings." Figure 11.2 is taken from the 2005 PepsiCo 10-K. This presentation is a little easier to pick out at the bottom of the Statement of Shareholders' Equity.

Comprehensive income and the components of other comprehensive income provide financial statement readers with more information than net income. Net income is important because it recognizes completed transactions. But comprehensive income—specifically, other comprehensive income—supplies information about future net income. Other comprehensive income reveals unfinished transactions, the unrealized gains and losses that will become realized and affect future net income.

Figure 11.2   Consolidated Statement of Common Shareholders' Equity

PepsiCo, Inc., and Subsidiaries
Fiscal Years Ended December 31, 2005,
December 25, 2004, and December 27, 2003

	(Dollars in Millions)			
	2005		**2004**	
	Shares	*Amount*	*Shares*	*Amount*
Common stock	1,782	$30	1,782	$30
Capital excess of par value				
Balance, beginning of year		618		548
Stock-based compensation expense		311		368
Stock option exercises		(315)		(298)
Balance, end of year		614		618
Retained earnings				
Balance, beginning of year		18,730		15,961
Net income		4,078		4,212
Cash dividends declared— common		(1,684)		(1,438)
Cash dividends declared— preferred		(3)		(3)
Cash dividends declared— RSUs		(5)		(2)
Other		—		—
Balance, end of year		21,116		18,730
Accumulated other comprehensive loss				
Balance, beginning of year		(886)		(1,267)
Currency translation adjustment		(251)		401
Cash flow hedges, net of tax:				
Net derivative gains/(losses)		54		(16)
Reclassification of (gains)/losses to net income		(8)		9
Minimum pension liability adjustment, net of tax		16		(19)
Unrealized gain on securities, net of tax		24		6
Other		(2)		—
Balance, end of year		(1,053)		(886)

STOCK ACCOUNT PLOYS

THE STOCK ACCOUNTS are not usually considered high risk for fraud, but a few classification and valuation issues can result in a murky picture of the equity of the company. The stock accounts are part of the equity section on the balance sheet and represent investments by stockholders. The stock is on the books at the price received at the original sale and is not adjusted for market value changes.

Ploy #1: Calling a Financial Instrument "Stock" When It Is Really Debt

It isn't always possible to categorize a balance sheet item by its name. Companies can issue stock that has all the characteristics

---

QUICK POINTS: STOCK ACCOUNT PLOYS

- ✧ Stock accounts are not at high risk for fraudulent financial reporting.
- ✧ The classification of some financial instruments can be tricky, with debt instruments being called "stock."
- ✧ A valuation problem may result if stock is sold for something other than cash.
- ✧ Issuing stock for a receivable means no cash is taken in, defeating the purpose of issuing stock.
- ✧ The stock option backdating scandal illustrates how companies circumvented the rules and the signs of that deception.

---

of a loan. The dividends are cumulative and stated as a percentage of par value, which seems like interest on a loan. The difference, though, is that dividends are not guaranteed or legally required, as is the interest. Instead, the cumulative feature brings unpleasant consequences for the company issuing the stock and not paying the dividends. The so-called stock can also have a feature called *mandatory redeemable stock*, which requires the issuer to buy back the stock by a certain date at a certain price. It seems that mandatory redeemable stock with a cumulative dividend is really a loan in disguise. The redeemable price is similar to repayment, and the dividends are similar to interest.

Classifying something like mandatory redeemable stock as equity rather than a debt or liability has advantages. Key ratios improve as debt decreases, signaling a more solvent company. For example, debt to total assets uses total liabilities in the numerator and total assets in the denominator. The incentive is to classify things not as debt to improve the ratio. That classification, though, misrepresents the obligations of the company. No debt is on the balance sheet for the required buyback of the stock, and users of the financial statements don't have the full story about the company's solvency.

To counteract this problem, accounting rules require that companies put things like mandatory redeemable stock on the balance sheet, but not in the stockholders' equity section, even though it is called stock. Instead, it is usually listed after liabilities but before the equity section.

Ploy #2: Receiving Noncash Assets in Exchange for Stock

A company issues stock for the purpose of receiving capital to take advantage of new opportunities, expand operations, or undertake other activities requiring additional cash. For this reason, most stock is issued for cash. It is unusual, but companies can issue stock for notes or stock subscriptions receivable. Such a ploy is really questionable. First, no additional cash is available. Second, earnings per share is diluted. Issuing stock without receiving cash doesn't make much sense.

Occasionally, however, a company may issue stock in exchange for goods or services. An example of this is an attorney exchanging legal services for stock or the owner of a vehicle exchanging the vehicle for shares of stock. If the stock is regularly traded and the market price is current, the value is established by the market value of the quantity of shares of stock issued. If, however, the stock is thinly traded and no current market price exists, the exchange of noncash goods or services can involve a valuation problem. Companies are required to disclose significant noncash transactions on the Statement of Cash Flows. Careful scrutiny of the description of those transactions will provide clues to the propriety of the valuation.

Ploy #3: The Great Stock Option Scandal

In order to understand the problem, we need to review the proper treatment of stock options. After defining stock options and how they work, we'll investigate how such options appear in the financial statements. Then we'll probe the activities that seem to be outside at least the spirit of the rules. Finally, we'll identify the clues and where to look to spot problems in your investments.

Stock options work like this. The compensation committee, part of the board of directors, grants the options in accordance with board policy. On a particular date, an employee receives the option to buy shares of stock at a given price over a specified period of time. The goal for the company is to motivate the employee to work hard and make good decisions that increase the stock price, which brings wealth to the stockholders. The goal for the employee is to make the share price increase so that when exercising the option, the employee pays less than the market price, resulting in a gain for the employee. That gain is a form of compensation. To illustrate this, assume an employee was granted an option to buy 5,000 shares of stock at $10 a share within a certain time frame. During that time, the stock increases to $20 a share, and the employee decides to exercise the option. The employee now has a gain of $50,000 (5,000 shares × $10 gain per share).

Normally, companies must record compensation expense on the income statement, but prior to 2004, rarely was there an expense for the compensation associated with stock options. That's because if the given price specified in the option was equal to the market price on the date the option was granted to the employee, the option was viewed as not having value—hence, zero compensation expense. Logically, though, that doesn't make any sense, because stock options were highly prized by employees and widely used to get and keep top talent, particularly in high-tech firms in the 1990s. If options had no value, why did employees accept them, and even desire them?

Recognizing that not recording compensation expense for options overstated income, accounting rule makers tried to change the accounting to require an expense for stock options, but they were unsuccessful prior to 1995, when the expensing of stock options became optional. Finally, in 2004, the expensing became mandatory. But by then some academic researchers were finding disturbing patterns in the dating of options.

Stock options were supposed to be the magic form of compensation that perfectly aligned the goals of employees and owners. Both would benefit from an increase in stock price, and the benefit would be in proportion to the amount of increase. The options usually set the option price as the market price the day before the grant or the day of the grant. Interestingly, academic researchers found that many times, the grant date was the same date as the lowest stock price of the year. This phenomenon suggested two things. First, the employees were guaranteed a paper gain and the incentive to increase the stock price was not as strong. All the employee had to do was maintain the stock price until the exercise date. Second, even under the old accounting rules, companies should have been recording compensation expense. Income was overstated when options were backdated.

The opportunity to backdate options existed because companies did not have to report the granting of options in a timely manner. Compensation committees could consider when to set the grant date after looking at the stock price movement. For example, on June 30, the committee decides to award stock options to executives. Board policy states that the option price is set at the closing price on the day before the options are granted. On June 29 the stock price closes at $45. Reviewing the stock prices, the committee finds that the low point for the previous six months was $34 on May 7. Somehow the papers are prepared showing the grant date of the options as May 8. Either the committee colludes with this backdating or it doesn't catch the date change. The effect, though, is that each option has a built-in paper gain of $11. The option grant report lists May 8 as the grant date, and that report is filed on July 1. In 2002, Sarbanes-Oxley requirements forced companies to report options within two days of the grant, reducing the time for backdating to two days. To comply with the new regulation, the earliest grant date allowed in the example would be June 27, using the June 26 closing price for the stock.

Although the two-day reporting rule limits backdating, it doesn't limit a practice called *springloading*. Instead of looking back in time to find a low point for the stock price, the grant date could be set just ahead of a planned announcement of good news or just after a planned announcement of bad news. In either case, the holder of the option would experience a probable increase in the value of the option. There is evidence that Apple Computers has been involved in the practices of springloading and backdating stock options since 1997. Apple is in the process of restating a number of years of financial data. While some argue that this is not illegal because there is no victim who loses, it smacks of acting on inside information, which is illegal.

Accounting rules require companies to disclose information about stock options. That information should help users understand the stock options that existed during the period covered by the income statement, including the compensation cost, cash flow effects, and the effect on shareholders of the options. But those disclosure requirements did not prevent the backdating. Some advocates are pushing for more disclosure, including telling shareholders the grant dates of options awarded during the year and the compensation committee meeting dates. That information could provide clues to backdating or springloading if the grant dates are removed from the meeting dates. Another clue to option manipulation is the timely filing of the required SEC form. The new rules require filing within two days, but not all companies file on time. Academic research found evidence of backdating in companies that filed late.

The stock accounts usually don't support fraud, but they may reflect some deceptive reporting practices. Readers of the financial statements need to understand the different types of stock issued by the company to identify any that act like debt, requiring cash flows similar to debt. That will include items on the balance sheet that go by the title "stock," but are not listed in the stockholders' equity section. That is the first clue that the element is not really an equity instrument. In addition to classification issues, valuation issues can plague the stock accounts. The equity section of the balance sheet and the notes contain information explaining any existing stock options, but that information is not enough to detect all the deceptive practices surrounding stock options. Only honest, attentive members of the board of directors and compensation committee can do that.

CHAPTER 13

RETAINED EARNINGS EVIDENCE

FINANCIAL STATEMENT USERS need to understand what the account titled "retained earnings" represents and how the balance changes. It is also important to understand the effect of various stock option transactions on retained earnings. Fortunately, recent changes to accounting rules closed one of the opportunities to hide expenses by an adjustment to retained earnings.

What Is Retained Earnings?

The retained earnings account in stockholders' equity on the balance sheet represents exactly what the title says—the earnings that have been retained in the company. The dollar amount in retained earnings is equal to the sum of all the net incomes earned

---

QUICK POINTS: RETAINED EARNINGS EVIDENCE

✧ Retained earnings is the accumulation of all the earnings of the company that have not been distributed to owners as dividends.
✧ The normal way to increase retained earnings is to earn a net profit for the accounting period.
✧ The normal way to decrease retained earnings is to earn a net loss for the accounting period or to give stockholders dividends.
✧ Transactions involving issuing stock for employee stock options can reduce retained earnings.

---

by the company less any dividends paid to owners over the life of the company. Each accounting period, retained earnings is increased by the amount of net income and decreased by the amount of dividends declared. Readers of the financial statements find this information in the Statement of Stockholders' Equity.

Sometimes a company will have several years of net losses, not income, and the retained earnings account may have a negative balance. A retained earnings account with a negative balance is called a *retained deficit.* Although it doesn't seem logical, a company can remain in business even if the balance sheet shows a retained deficit because a retained deficit is not the same as cash. A retained deficit does not represent an overdrawn checking account. It is only an accumulation of all earnings, losses, and distributions to owners from the beginning of the business. The same reasoning leads us to realize that retained earnings does not equal the amount of cash on hand. A comparison between the cash balance and the retained earnings balance on the balance sheet reveals that they are almost never the same amount.

The retained earnings account isn't cash, but it does indicate the amount available for dividends. It is important to note, though, that a company couldn't pay dividends in the amount of retained earnings unless it had enough cash to do so. To send a clearer signal about the amount of retained earnings that can be distributed through dividends, companies may partition retained earnings. Identifying part of retained earnings as "appropriated" means that it is not for distribution. Often the appropriated retained earnings will inform the reader of the purpose for the partition— for example, a future investment. A search of SEC filings found that appropriated retained earnings appeared most often in the statements of foreign companies.

While some appropriations of retained earnings are the result of company decisions, sometimes companies have restrictions imposed on them. Loan agreements or bond covenants may require companies to maintain a minimum level of capital, and companies can restrict retained earnings to comply with those debt covenants provisions. Within retained earnings, amounts that are restricted or appropriated are not available for distribution as dividends.

What Other Changes Occur in Retained Earnings?

Information about changes in all the accounts in the stockholders' equity section of the balance sheet is available on the Statement of Stockholders' Equity. The traditional format for that statement uses a column for each account in the stockholders' equity section. The top line is the beginning balance in each account. Items causing changes in those accounts are listed on the left side. Decreases in the accounts are denoted in parentheses. Figure 13.1 is a simplified version of a Statement of Stockholders' Equity for a fictitious company. It gives you an idea of the format of the statement.

Companies that award stock options will usually have a decrease in retained earnings resulting from the sale of treasury stock. That reduction is a cost of using stock options as compensation. Here is how it happens. A company has a limited number of shares of stock that it can issue. To have enough shares to sell to employees wanting to exercise options, the company will buy back its own shares in the market. Those shares are called *trea-*

Figure 13.1

KAMKEM, Inc. Statement of Stockholders' Equity			
	(Dollars in Millions)		
	Common Stock and Additional Paid-in Capital	*Retained Earnings*	*Treasury Stock*	*Total*
Balance 12/31/06	$250.00	$100.00		$350.00
Net income		20.00		20.00
Cash dividends declared		(1.00)		(1.00)
Common stock issued	10.00			10.00
Treasury stock purchase and sales		(19.00)	($40.00)	($59.00)
Balance 12/31/07	$260.00	$100.00	($40.00)	$320.00

sury stock, and the company must pay the market price to acquire them. Then, when the company issues those shares in the exercise of stock options, if the option price is less than the market price, the difference directly reduces retained earnings if no other treasury stock capital accounts exist. When reviewing the Statement of Stockholders' Equity, a reduction in retained earnings related to treasury stock transactions usually means that the exercise of stock options required the company to purchase stock in the market and turn around and issue it to the option holder.

How Do Changes in Accounting Principle Affect Retained Earnings?

Until 2005, managers had a particularly tricky way of avoiding expenses on the income statement. They could decide to change the method of accounting and avoid the expense completely because accounting rules allowed the adjustment for the change to be a one-time charge that showed up as a change in the beginning retained earnings balance. This treatment made it easy to miss, and the result was that some expenses never appeared on the income statement, giving a murky picture of performance and efficiency.

Companies must now use the retrospective method of reporting changes in accounting principle, changing from one correct way of accounting to another correct method. While still requiring an adjustment to retained earnings for the earliest year presented, the retrospective method requires the company to also adjust all the financial statements shown in the annual report to the way they would appear if the new method had been used. This means that all the balance sheet accounts and income statement accounts for the years shown for comparison must be recalculated. Hewlett-Packard's 2005 annual report included income statement information for three years and balance sheet information for two years. Although costly, it is now more difficult to have expenses bypass the income statement.

PART IV

UNCOVERING CLUES ON THE BALANCE SHEET

CHAPTER 14

ASSET SCAMS

Assets are things of value owned by the company, and they exist in several forms. Tangible assets are things like cash, inventory, or equipment. Intangible assets can be rights to use or receive something, like accounts receivable, trademarks, or copyrights. Intangible assets can also be just a calculated amount resulting from the purchase of another company, called *goodwill*. Asset scams usually involve overstating the value. In some cases, the classification of the asset can make a big difference in income.

Quick Points: Asset Scams

- ❖ Assets are defined as future economic benefits owned by a company.
- ❖ Current assets may be overstated, misleading investors into thinking the company has higher liquidity than it does:
  - ❖ Cash on the balance sheet may include compensating balances that really aren't available for use.
  - ❖ Cash equivalents are liquid investments such as money market funds and are included in the cash balance.
  - ❖ Accounts receivable are overstated if the estimate for uncollectible accounts is too low.
  - ❖ Inventory may include the value of obsolete items that won't sell.
  - ❖ Inventory write-downs are listed as a one-time charge instead of being identified as operating expenses.
- ❖ Property and equipment amounts can be increased above the original cost by capitalizing expenses.

- ❖ Two classifications of investments are not on the balance sheet at market value, and management decides when a decline in value is permanent, requiring a reduction in the balance sheet value:
  - ❖ Debt securities classified as held-to-maturity are carried at the present value of the maturity value.
  - ❖ Equity method investments are a calculated amount that is unrelated to market value.
- ❖ Intangible asset values can be misleading in two ways:
  - ❖ Assets like patents and copyrights, although legally still enforceable, may not be equal to the balance sheet value.
  - ❖ Goodwill is written down only when management determines the value is impaired.
- ❖ Investors can detect asset scams through ratios and quantitative analysis.
- ❖ Investors, by reading the notes carefully, can find information on policies that affect asset valuation.

Scam #1: Inflating Current Asset Values

Current assets represent cash or near cash available for paying bills or distributions to shareholders. Most companies want more current assets rather than fewer, to present improved liquidity. For that reason, investors need to watch for inflated current asset values.

The normal term on the balance sheet is *cash and cash equivalents*, and that includes some cash amounts that aren't available for use. For example, cash may consist of not only cash in checking accounts but also minimum required account balances. Lines of credit may also require a minimum balance in an account. Is that cash included in the amount of cash on the balance sheet? Actually, it might be on the face of the balance sheet, so it is important to read the note disclosure. The SEC requires companies to disclose the amount of minimum required account balances, also called *compensating balances*, if that amount is larger than 15 percent of the total of cash and marketable securities. That means up to 15 percent of the cash and cash equivalents balance may be restricted. In that case, cash is overvalued. The investor can find information on compensating balances in the notes to the financial statements if the amount is 15 percent or more.

Cash equivalents are sometimes called *near money* and consist of things like money market funds and Treasury bills. Inflated values for cash equivalents occur if the instruments classified as cash equivalents are not easily liquidated.

Accounts receivable, another current asset on the balance sheet, are very susceptible to inflated valuation because the reported amount is based on an estimate of the amount of receivables that won't be collected. The amount of that estimate is disclosed, but that estimate is subject to judgment and based on historical patterns of nonpayment. This works just fine if the customer profile remains the same, but if a company begins to increase revenues by selling to less creditworthy customers, the payments will not follow the old pattern and the estimate will be too low.

Inventory valuation is tricky. Accounting rules allow lots of flexibility in valuing this asset, but if done consistently, comparison from one year to the next is valid and understandable. If the amount increases, you know it is because the quantity of items in inventory increased, the cost of each item in inventory increased, or there was a combination of increases in both price and quantity. That comparison isn't clear if the company changes its method of valuing inventory. Luckily, the company must disclose in the notes to the financial statements how it measures inventory.

Another issue in inventory valuation is the choice of cost flow. The common alternatives are LIFO and FIFO, which are acronyms for "last-in-first-out" and "first-in-first-out," respectively. LIFO usually results in a higher cost of sales and lower inventory value on the balance sheet than FIFO.

A difficult problem for investors is determining whether the inventory is salable. The cost of inventory that is old and difficult to sell may be included in the balance sheet value for inventory, and that would overstate its value. Relying on audit procedures may not be enough. Auditors are required to physically view inventory to make sure it exists, but not every item is checked, and it can be easy for companies to perpetrate a fraud. Auditors must make unannounced inventory checks so that management doesn't just move items from warehouse to warehouse. Auditors must also check closed boxes to be sure they actually contain goods. The company may try to fool auditors into misjudging the quantity of good inventory. Then, supposing some of the inventory is obsolete, figuring out exactly when to write off obsolete inventory is an art not a science. The one-time charge to write down inventory should be included in cost of goods sold, not as a special charge, and signals that previously reported margins were too high.

Inflating current asset value misleads investors into believing the company has more liquid assets than it really does. This means that it gives the impression that more cash is available for paying bills and paying dividends.

Scam #2: Boosting Property and Equipment Accounts

Long-term asset values are usually manipulated in two ways. The first is through add-ons after the purchase of the asset. Things like property and equipment usually have a specified price. All the costs to prepare the asset for service—such as delivery, setup, calibrating equipment, or remodeling a building—are capitalized, added to the cost, and reported on the balance sheet. After the purchase, the company may capitalize amounts it spends to repair or maintain the asset, increasing the reported value on the balance sheet. That capitalization has two positive results. First, the dollars spent do not decrease income all at once but are allocated through depreciation over a longer period of time, resulting in smoother earnings. Second, the total assets on the balance sheet increase, giving the impression of a stronger balance sheet.

For example, assume we have a delivery business. The largest group of assets on the balance sheet may be the fleet of delivery trucks. Those trucks need regular maintenance. That regular maintenance should be recorded as an operating expense because it is benefiting the current period. If one of the trucks needed a new engine, the cost of that new engine should be added to the value of the truck (capitalized) and depreciated over future periods because that new engine will benefit future periods. In this case, the cost of the regular maintenance may be quite substantial. If the earnings for the year are lower than expected, the company may capitalize those maintenance costs, which would increase the earnings for the year and spread those costs over future years.

The second way long-term asset values are manipulated is through ignoring a decrease in the value of the asset. If the value of the asset declines and the decline is judged to be permanent, the company must reduce the value of the asset and reduce income by the same amount. The accounting rules, however, allow for judgment as to the amount of the decline and the evaluation of the decline as permanent or temporary. That flexibility gives management room to postpone or speed up the write-off, depending on how big a hit earnings for the period can take and still meet expectations.

Scam #3: Pumping Income with Investments

Companies can classify investments as either trading securities, which are current assets, or other types of investments, which may be either current or long-term assets. The classification makes a big difference in the effect on income. Trading securities are investments, of any type, that the company intends to sell in the short term. Any changes in the market value of those investments are recognized in income immediately, even before the investment is sold. Companies can't really manipulate the results of trading securities.

Other classifications of investments are a different story. Available-for-sale investments may be either current assets or long-term assets, but either way, any change in market value is not recognized in income. The company must adjust the balance sheet amount to reflect the change in value, but the unrealized gain or loss does not affect income. Instead, it shows up as a component of other comprehensive income. When the investment is sold, the difference between the cost of the investment and the proceeds from the sale is a realized gain or loss that affects income. Companies can't manipulate the balance sheet value, but they can cherry-pick the investments, selling ones with gains and hanging on to the losers, to improve earnings for the period. Assume a company has two available-for-sale investments, each having a market value of $20,000 at year-end. If the first investment had a decline in value of $5,000 during the year and the second had a gain of $5,000 during the year, the company would choose to sell the second so that there would be a realized gain of $5,000 on the income statement. The unrealized loss on the first investment would not hit the income statement but would show up in other comprehensive income. Management could be motivated to hang on to a loser to avoid reducing income.

Two classifications of investments can present some valuation issues. Debt securities classified as held-to-maturity and equity method investments are not usually valued at market value on the balance sheet. In both classifications, accounting rules require a calculated value rather than a market value. The logic is that both investments are going to be long term and therefore market value is not a relevant attribute. Particularly in the case of debt securities classified as held-to-maturity, the balance sheet value represents the present value of the amount to be received at the maturity of the bond or other debt. Like all assets, though, both of these classifications are subject to write-down if the decline in value is thought to be permanent rather than temporary. This allows management the discretion to decide when the decline is permanent and they give up hope that the market price will increase. At that point the company must decrease the value of the investment, but that point may depend more on the level of earnings than on the nature of the decline in value.

Scam #4: Hanging On to Intangibles

Intangible assets consist of two broad categories. The first category is identifiable intangible assets, such as patents, copyrights, and trademarks, which have a useful life associated with the legal terms of the asset. The other category is goodwill, which arises when a company makes an acquisition and the purchase price exceeds the value of the net assets acquired. The only scam associated with identifiable intangible assets is the amortization period. Often the legal time period is longer than the useful life of a patent. This is particularly true for patents associated with technology or drugs. That makes the amortization expense too low and earnings too high, and the asset value on the balance sheet too high.

The real scam, though, is in the category of goodwill. New accounting rules for goodwill became effective in 2002. Prior to that, the cost of goodwill, calculated as the excess of the purchase price of an acquisition over the market value of the net assets, was amortized over a time period of 40 years or less. That time period seemed too long and arbitrary, so the new rules eliminated amortization completely. Instead, companies must annually test the goodwill for impairment of value and write down the value if it is found to be impaired. That impairment testing is another area of financial reporting that allows flexibility and judgment rather than precise rules. Companies may take the impairment charges when earnings can withstand the reduction rather than when the asset really is impaired.

Detection Technique: Ratios

Some quantitative techniques help investors check for asset scams such as overvalued accounts receivable. A comparison of the percentage increase in revenue to the percentage increase in receivables, net of any estimate for bad debts, will reveal changes in the credit quality of customers. A faster increase in receivables growth versus revenue growth indicates customers are paying more slowly. While that increased time to pay could be symptomatic of a common characteristic of customers, it could also signal a company that is increasing sales revenue by selling to customers with weaker credit profiles.

For example, in 2004 Navistar (formerly International Harvester) had a 28 percent increase in annual sales. Along with the sales increase, the company's receivables increased 30 percent. This difference in percentage increase should give investors a reason to investigate the company a little further.

Investigating increases in inventory can reveal inventory scams. A comparison of the increase in revenue to the increase in inventory can indicate trouble. If inventory is increasing faster than revenue, the company could be facing a slowdown in orders or have overvalued inventory. It is also a good idea to check the trend of change in gross profit margin. A big increase or decrease in the rate of change in profit margin, adjusting for seasonality, can signal inventory problems. (The aforementioned Navistar also had an increase in inventory of 33 percent during 2004 when its sales increased 28 percent.)

Another useful technique when comparing companies using different inventory cost flow methods is adjusting LIFO inventory to FIFO. Companies using LIFO must disclose the LIFO reserve amount in the notes. The LIFO reserve is the amount of the adjustment from LIFO to the company's internal reporting method, often FIFO. The investor can then use the LIFO reserve to convert the company's LIFO valued inventory to a rough approximation of FIFO by simply adding the reserve to the LIFO valued inventory. If a company's LIFO balance is $48,000 at the end of the year and in the notes the LIFO reserve is given as $5,000, the value of the inventory under FIFO would be $53,000. This also means, though, that the cost of goods sold (expense) would have been different for the fiscal year. Cost of goods sold is higher under LIFO when the cost of inventory is rising.

Detection Technique: Notes

Careful reading of the notes to the financial statements reveals all kinds of clues, and clues to asset scams are no exception. Cash and cash equivalent disclosure should present the details of the compensating balances and just what is included in cash equivalents. That information can let investors decide how much of the cash balance is really available cash.

Accounts receivable and the allowance for uncollectible accounts receive extensive disclosure in the notes, but to get the full picture it is necessary to compare with previous years' disclosures. Companies must disclose a change in bad debt estimate percentage in note 1. Increasing that estimate means it was too low in the past. That low estimate could be the result of an honest mistake due to an industrywide problem or it could be the result of bogus sales or decreasing credit quality of customers.

The notes also contain information on the company's method for capitalizing expenses. Careful evaluation of that policy can alert the investor to aggressive accounting that boosts the property and equipment accounts. Companies should capitalize only those expenditures that will benefit future operating periods.

In the notes, investors should read the sections pertaining to investments to find clues to the amount of impairment losses and the techniques the company uses to determine impairment losses. Investors can compare their company with others in the same industry to assess the normalcy of the techniques.

If a company falls into any of the situations dealing with assets that have been mentioned in this chapter, it does not mean that there is a scam in process. This information should alert investors to be cautious and to spend the time to investigate a company further.

CHAPTER 15

LIABILITY TRICKS

Liabilities are obligations of the company that are most often represented as debts that require cash to satisfy. Sometimes the company must provide goods or services to eliminate the liability. Liabilities classified as current liabilities are obligations that require payment within a year.

Investors are interested in two aspects of liabilities, other than due date. The first is existence. When reading the financial reports, you should feel confident that the company has listed all of its liabilities. The second aspect of interest is the measurement

---

Quick Points: Liability Tricks

- ❖ Companies can increase profit by failing to record or minimizing the estimate of liabilities.
- ❖ Companies can avoid recording liabilities by making favorable judgments after analyzing the situation.
- ❖ Accounting rules allow companies to avoid listing some liabilities.
- ❖ Many liabilities on the balance sheet are difficult to understand, obscuring their importance:
  - ❖ Pension liabilities.
  - ❖ Unearned revenue.
  - ❖ Deferred taxes.
- ❖ Detect liability tricks through ratio analysis.
- ❖ Discover liability tricks through careful reading of the notes and management discussion and analysis.

---

of liabilities. Investors need to know how much companies owe to predict the company's cash outflows.

Trick #1: Failing to Record Liabilities Associated with Regular Expenses

Several regularly occurring expenses, such as warranties and uncollectible accounts, are only estimates because the expense is recorded before the actual occurrence of the warranty work or before the account becomes uncollectible. Matching requires recording expenses on the same income statement as the revenue produced by them, even if that means estimating the amount of the expense. Although it is difficult to completely avoid recording liabilities for warranties and uncollectible accounts, the measurement issue is very real. These items are estimates, so management can manipulate the amounts through analysis.

At the end of the accounting period, companies record accrued expenses for unpaid expenses that should be recognized on the income statement. The accrual procedure to get the expense on the income statement results in accrued liabilities on the balance sheet. Things like salaries that employees have earned but not yet received, utility bills that relate to the accounting period but haven't been paid, and taxes that are an expense of the year but are not due until later are common examples of accrued liabilities. Some accrued liabilities, such as the examples given, undeniably exist and are easy to measure. Many accrued liabilities involve much more management judgment and provide opportunities for earnings manipulation.

Trick #2: Favorable Analysis Means No Liability Recorded for Unusual Situations

In some instances, companies can avoid recording even the existence of certain liabilities. Management must use judgment to decide on the recording of contingencies and some types of long-term contracts.

Contingent liabilities are obligations that may or may not come to pass. Management must analyze the probabilities of the event happening. If the likelihood of the event occurring is probable, then the company records a loss and a liability. If the event doesn't meet the threshold for recording—in other words, it is only possible, not probable—then no liability is put on the financial statements. Instead, management must disclose the contingency in the notes. An example of a contingent liability is a lawsuit. If the company is involved in a lawsuit and feels that it is "reasonably possible" that there will be an unfavorable outcome, it is required to disclose this lawsuit in a footnote. But if it is "probable" that the outcome will be unfavorable and the company is able to reasonably estimate the amount, a liability would have to be recorded. Another example of a contingent liability that has footnote disclosure only is self-insurance. If a company is self-insured against some event (fire, flood), it will disclose this in a footnote and not record the liability until the event occurs. The analysis of the probabilities drives the recognition of the liability. Contingent assets or gains are not recognized until they actually happen.

Trick #3: Making the Liabilities Difficult to Understand

The definition of a liability states that it is a probable future outflow or sacrifice of resources that obligates a company as a result of a past event, and investors often think that means debts. But the balance sheet has some unusual liabilities that aren't the same as borrowings. The names and measurement of these liabilities can be tricky.

Most large companies have a pension plan for employees. While fewer and fewer have a defined-benefit plan, many companies have had pension plans that guarantee certain benefits to employees. For example, most of the big car companies not only have plans that guarantee a certain amount of benefit, they also have plans that guarantee the provision of health care. However, companies do not have to record a liability for the value of those guaranteed benefits. Instead, companies must record as a liability the difference between the assets that back the pension plan and the present value of all benefits earned so far. The measurement of this liability is related to a present-value calculation. Management can manipulate the present-value calculation through the choice of discount rate. The higher the discount rate, the lower the present value and the less likely the company will record an additional pension liability.

Other confusing liabilities include the category of unearned revenue. Unearned revenue is a liability that arises when a customer pays ahead for a product or service. Although unearned revenue, also called *deferred revenue,* is a good thing because it represents soon-to-be-earned income, it is a liability because the company has the obligation to provide products or services that the customer has already paid for. Microsoft has unearned revenue relating to software updates. When customers buy a software package, they are entitled to updates for the software. As those updates are distributed, that liability is satisfied and Microsoft earns the revenue. Some cases of unearned revenue are more complex than the software example. Stores that sell gift certificates can't recognize the revenue until the certificate is redeemed or the certificate expires. Airlines must account for the obligation associated with frequent-flyer miles, usually through deferred revenue by allocating a portion of the ticket price to a liability.

Many companies record deferred tax amounts because of differences between financial reporting requirements and the tax code. For example, a company records an expense for depreciation that is often different from the depreciation deduction allowed on the tax return. Usually, the tax code allows for larger deductions for depreciation than a company takes on the income statement. The difference between the two amounts is only temporary and gives rise to a deferred tax liability.

For example, assume the depreciation for an asset under the tax code is $5,000 and for the financial statements is $3,000. Using a 40 percent tax rate, the deferred tax liability on this asset would be $800 [($5,000 – $3,000) × 40%]. This $800 in tax will have to be paid eventually when the depreciation expense under the tax code is lower than the depreciation expense on the financial statements.

Trick #4: Unrecorded Liabilities

Not all obligations meet the threshold for recording a liability. Many long-term contracts are disclosed only in the notes. Financial reporting rules establish criteria for recording liabilities for leases and purchase commitments, and companies carefully construct the deals to avoid reporting the liabilities.

Certain purchase commitment contracts are not recorded as liabilities, even though the company is locked into purchasing a specified quantity at a specified price. The only disclosure for most of these contracts occurs when the company experiences a loss.

For example, Ford had a contract to purchase a metal—palladium—used in catalytic converters. During 2001, the price fell by more than 50 percent and engineering advances reduced the need for the metal, requiring Ford to record a $953 million loss on the contract. That was quite a surprise for investors because no liability for the purchase contract had been on the 2000 balance sheet or in the note disclosures, beyond general references to hedging commodities.

Leases may or may not be recognized as liabilities, depending on the terms. Current accounting rules provide a list of four criteria and if the lease meets any one of the criteria, it is recorded as a capital lease. Capital leases are treated like a purchase over time and require including both the leased asset and the liability for payments on the books. If, however, the lease avoids meeting the criteria, no liability, or asset, is recorded. Only note disclosure alerts investors to the existence of the lease obligation.

Companies that issue stock options to their executives also carry an unrecorded liability. When employees exercise their options, they pay less than the market price for stock. The company receives the cash, uses it to buy back shares of stock in the market, and then issues the shares to the employee. Stock options put a burden on existing shareholders, either through less cash available for distribution or lower earnings per share. The problem is that the cash to buy back shares needed to meet the demand for the exercise of the stock options is less than the cash received from the employees. To buy back the number of shares needed for the option exercise, the company must use its own cash, reducing the amount available for distribution as dividends. If the company does not buy back the same number of shares as it issues, the earnings per share goes down because more shares are outstanding.

Investors are concerned with a company's liability for future cash outflows. It aids in predicting future profitability. To do that analysis, the financial statements must report the liabilities and provide a meaningful measure of the obligation. Current accounting rules allow for judgment in determining the existence and in measurement of liabilities, and investors need to know the tricks to accurately evaluate the prospects of the companies in their portfolio.

Detection Technique: Ratios and Trends

Tracking trends in various liability accounts can help investors spot problems. The warranty liability should change in the same way and at the same rate as sales. Two explanations exist for a situation in which the warranty liability is increasing at a rate faster than sales. The company could be padding the liability by increasing the associated expense, shifting future expenses into the current periods. The other explanation is equally as bad. The company finds increasing warranty costs necessary because product quality is slipping, thus requiring more after-sale service. A change in the opposite direction from sales doesn't make any sense and suggests the company is manipulating expenses through the warranty liability. The allowance for uncollectible accounts should also present the same trend as sales.

The trend of accrued liabilities is particularly useful for spotting earnings management because of the amount of management judgment involved in establishing the existence and the amounts of the expenses associated with these liabilities. The rate of change in accrued liabilities should be similar to the rate of change in sales revenue over a year. Changes from one quarter to the next do not signal problems. A decline in accrued liabilities means that the company has made more payments than it has recorded new expenses. Another check related to accrued liabilities is to compare the percentage of general, selling, and administrative expenses as a percentage of revenue over time. If the percentage goes down, it can indicate either more efficiency, resulting in lower operating expenses, or that the company is minimizing the accrual of expenses.

Detection Technique: Careful Reading of the Financial Reports

The management discussion and analysis (MD&A) section of the company's annual report is the first place to look for liability tricks. The MD&A section of the 2004 IBM annual report explains the increase in the warranty liability accrual as "primarily related to personal computers resulting from increased volumes," a logical increase.

The second place to find information on liability tricks is in the notes to the financial statements. The first note on accounting policies will explain the method of estimating accruals for warranties and bad debts. That note should also describe the composition of selling, general, and administrative expenses. Watch for changes in the methods or composition because that may signal earnings manipulation.

CHAPTER 16

CLASSIFICATION DECEIT

THIS CHAPTER FOCUSES on the importance of classification on the balance sheet. In particular, we look at the distinction between current and noncurrent assets and liabilities to understand the importance of that classification. Then, discussion of investment classification highlights the income effects of classification decisions. Finally, we look at the treatment of leases and the consequences of categorizing a lease transaction as an operating versus a capital lease.

QUICK POINTS: CLASSIFICATION DECEIT

- ⬥ Both assets and liabilities are classified as either current or noncurrent:
    - ⬥ Current assets are cash or will become cash within the next year.
    - ⬥ Current liabilities are obligations that will require the use of current assets to satisfy the obligation or the creation of another current liability.
- ⬥ Companies can classify current liabilities as noncurrent if assets are set aside for the payment of the liability.
- ⬥ Companies can classify investments in several different ways, and the classification affects not only the balance sheet but the income statement, too.
- ⬥ Leases classified as operating leases avoid appearing on the balance sheet completely.

What Balance Sheet Classifications Exist for Assets and Liabilities?

Both assets and liabilities can be classified as either current or noncurrent, depending on the time period associated with the transformation into cash or satisfaction of the obligation. Assets are, according to the official FASB definition, "probable future economic benefits obtained or controlled by a particular entity as a result of past transactions or events." Examples are cash, inventories, land, and patents. Generally, assets are things of value, economic resources that are useful in the business operations. For an asset to be classified as a current asset, the company that controls it must be able to convert it to cash within a year or the operating cycle, whichever is longer. Cash is a current asset and doesn't have to be converted. Inventory is a current asset that is sold to customers who will pay cash either immediately or in a short period of time. A company would prefer to have more current assets than fewer in most situations.

Any asset that is not classified as current is a noncurrent asset. The balance sheet doesn't usually have a noncurrent asset category but lists them separately after the current assets. Examples of noncurrent assets are property, plant, and equipment, intangible assets, and a category called "other assets." Companies usually allocate the cost of noncurrent assets to expense over time, with the exception of goodwill and deferred tax assets. Goodwill, an intangible asset, is not amortized. Instead, companies must write down the value of goodwill if analysis shows it to be worth less than the balance sheet value. The amount of the write-down reduces income. Deferred tax assets represent tax savings from future tax deductions. Deferred tax assets are not amortized, but they may have a valuation allowance attached that reduces the value, if analysis shows the company may not have income sufficient to use all the future deductions.

Liabilities are, again according to the official FASB definition, "probable future economic sacrifices obligating a particular entity as a result of a past transaction." Often liabilities are debts and are classified as current or noncurrent depending on the due date of the payoff. Current liabilities are obligations that the company must pay or otherwise satisfy within a year or the operating cycle, whichever is longer. Anything not due in a year is noncurrent. Usually companies would prefer to classify debt as noncurrent rather than current to boost liquidity.

Why Do Companies Fiddle with Classifications?

Ratio analysis relies on numbers from the balance sheet and uses numbers based on the classification as current or noncurrent assets or liabilities. Managers want to make the ratios look better, giving the company a higher stock price and access to more capital.

For example, the current ratio is equal to the total current assets divided by the total current liabilities. The ratio obviously should be greater than 1. By classifying a current liability as noncurrent, the ratio improves.

How Can Companies Fiddle with Classifications?

Companies are supposed to classify any debt due in the next year as a current liability. There is an out, though, if the company has funds set aside for the repayment. Those funds must be classified as a noncurrent asset. Only footnote disclosure reveals the certain reduction of long-term debt through the use of noncurrent assets.

Companies fiddle with the classification of investments. An investment can be either a current or a noncurrent asset, depending on when management intends to sell it. If sale is anticipated within a year, the investment is a current asset. If management intends to hold the investment longer than a year, then the investment is noncurrent. Management's intent determines the classification.

The financial reporting rules for investments depend on another set of classifications. Investments can be classified as trading securities, available-for-sale securities, and held-to-maturity securities. Changes in the value of trading securities are recognized in income even before the investment is sold. Changes in the value of available-for-sale investments are reported on the balance sheet, but they are included only as a component of other comprehensive income and do not affect net income until the investment is actually sold. Changes in the market value of investments in held-to-maturity securities are ignored. That means the same security could appear three different ways in the financial statements, depending on management's intent and classification.

Investors must read all the financial disclosures about investments very carefully to understand the classification scheme management is using. Be wary of companies that reclassify investments often. That could be a sign of manipulation of earnings. Also, not many companies outside of financial institutions use the trading security classification. If a company in your portfolio does, watch for the unrealized gains from increases in the value of trading securities. Those gains will be real only when the investment is sold.

Leases provide management with another opportunity to fiddle with the classification of items on the balance sheet. Lease accounting is complicated and often disguises a financed purchase rather than the temporary use of an asset. The international accounting rule makers are studying the requirement to record all leases as financed purchases rather than operating leases.

Lease accounting is under scrutiny after recent problems at Krispy Kreme. In 2002 Krispy Kreme set up a lease to finance a new $30 million dough-mixing plant in Illinois. This lease kept the debt off the balance sheet, off-balance-sheet financing. Krispy Kreme disclosed this lease arrangement in its quarterly reports. Because of the Enron debacle and off-balance-sheet financing, analysts and regulators looked at the arrangement much more closely. This arrangement was publicized by analysts through the media, and the stock price fell. Krispy Kreme decided to change its method of financing the purchase and put it back on the balance sheet.

Investors can find information on a company's lease obligations in the notes to the financial statements. Operating leases represent long-term liabilities that do not appear on the balance sheet but are disclosed in the notes.

CHAPTER 17

OFF-BALANCE-SHEET SHAMS

ALTHOUGH USERS OF financial statements can find clues to aggressive and fraudulent accounting *on* the balance sheet, there may be important things that are *not on* the balance sheet. Most of the time these important things are debts, and omitting them from the balance sheet makes the company look better. Less debt means the company has more financial flexibility. Less debt means fewer cash outflows for repayment and interest and more cash available for dividends. The pretense misleads investors, and new rules make it more difficult to engage in the charade.

QUICK POINTS: OFF-BALANCE-SHEET SHAMS

✧ Off-balance-sheet financing can reduce the amount of debt on the balance sheet.
✧ Leases may or may not show up on the balance sheet of a company.
✧ Special-purpose entities were used in the past to remove debt from a company's balance sheet.
✧ New accounting rules regarding variable-interest entities (the new name for special-purpose entities) make it more difficult to accomplish off-balance-sheet financing.
✧ Readers of financial statements can't detect all off-balance-sheet shams, but the notes either disclose or hint at them.

Sham #1: Leases

In business, a lease is often a disguised purchase. A company needing the use of a building or equipment could get a loan and buy the asset. The result would be increased assets and increased debt on the balance sheet that would adversely affect some key financial ratios. Financially strong companies can weather the negative effect on ratios, but companies in a weaker position can't. Still needing the building or equipment for operations, the company can decide to avoid the problems of additional debt and instead lease the asset.

A true lease involves the temporary use of an asset. Creative businesspeople designed a lease transaction that involved terms such as automatic transfer of title at the end of the lease, or an opportunity to buy the asset at the end of the lease for a small amount, or a lease so long that neither the owner of the asset nor the lessee cared about ownership because the asset was used up. To counteract these sham leases, the accounting rules established clear, quantitative criteria for classifying leases. If the transaction doesn't meet any of the criteria, the lease is an operating lease, a true lease, and the lessee doesn't have to show the asset or the obligation on the balance sheet. If the transaction meets any one of the criteria, the lease is a capital lease and is accounted for just like a purchase from the owner, with the lease acting as financing. The lessee must record the asset and the liability for the asset.

The problem is that the lease rules provide specific quantitative criteria for determining classification. This allows companies to carefully structure lease deals to avoid meeting the criteria and keep the debt off the balance sheet.

Sham #2: Special-Purpose Entities and Variable-Interest Entities

Special-purpose entities were used extensively by Enron to hide the financing necessary for the many acquisitions it made to demonstrate the high growth rate. Clever names, like Raptor and Chewco, were given to partnerships that were presented as independent but really were set up, controlled, and capitalized by Enron. The old rules allowed companies to exclude special-purpose entities from their books if the outside capitalization was 3 percent or more. This means that Company A could contribute $97,000 to a partnership and another party could contribute $3,000. The partnership would buy an asset using some of the $100,000 as a down payment and arrange financing for the remainder of the cost. Because the partnership has no other debt and lots of cash, it is easy to get a loan at a good rate. Then, the partnership turns around and leases the asset to Company A, careful to construct an operating lease that requires no balance sheet debt. The lease payments fund the debt. The result is that Company A has the use of the asset at a lower rate than if it had obtained its own financing and no trace of the loan on the balance sheet, tricking investors into thinking it has fewer obligations than it does.

Enron went even further, though, and figured out a way to help the other, 3 percent investor get the necessary cash to invest in the partnership. Enron "sold" the investor Enron stock, but the investor didn't have to pay immediately because Enron took a receivable for the payment. Effectively, Enron was financing the entire partnership.

Post-Enron, new accounting rules have made it more difficult to accomplish this, but off-balance-sheet vehicles still exist, only now they are called *variable-interest entities* (VIEs) or *qualified special-purpose entities* (QSPEs). The new rules require determining which party really controls the variable-interest entity through complicated analysis of which party gets the rewards or takes the risks associated with the entity. And the rules raised the required outside investment amount to 10 percent. But only the primary beneficiary, the party that is determined to take the majority of the risk, must include the assets and debts of the VIE or QSPE. Because the rules specify "majority," not every VIE will have a primary beneficiary, allowing off-balance-sheet financing.

Detection Technique: Careful Reading of MD&A and the Notes

In 2003, the SEC issued new rules regarding the disclosure of off-balance-sheet arrangements. Management discussion and analysis (MD&A) must include a separate section, clearly labeled, that presents information on any such arrangements. The SEC rule requires disclosure of obligations associated with any contracts in a tabular format. The easiest way to find this information in the MD&A is to look for the labeled section and for a table of information. Another option is to use an annual report in PDF format, often available on the company's website, usually under the investor relations section. With that annual report or 10-K filing in a PDF format, you can use a search function looking for the term "variable-interest entity," "primary beneficiary," "consolidation," or "lease." That search should result in a number of spots in the filing that provide information on possible off-balance-sheet shams.

PART V

SPOTTING CLUES IN THE NOTES TO THE FINANCIAL STATEMENTS

CHAPTER 18

SIGNIFICANT ACCOUNTING POLICIES AND CHANGES IN THEM

INVESTORS USUALLY BELIEVE financial reports are based on hard-and-fast rules. As seen in previous chapters, many times financial results are influenced by choices and judgments that management makes about reporting options. In this chapter we consider how investors can learn more about the accounting policy choices and what happens when companies change a policy.

QUICK POINTS: ACCOUNTING POLICIES AND CHANGES IN THEM

- ✧ Companies have choices in how to report things in the financial statements.
- ✧ Companies must disclose information about accounting policies in several places in the annual report:
  - ✧ MD&A contains required disclosures about accounting policies.
  - ✧ The first note deals with significant accounting policies.
- ✧ Companies can choose to change from one correct accounting method to another.
- ✧ New rules effective in 2006 eliminated the cumulative effect of change in accounting principle on the face of the income statement.
- ✧ A change in accounting principle requires the company to fix any historical information in the annual report to reflect the new method.
- ✧ Accounting changes are easy to confuse with the correction of errors.
- ✧ Restatements from changes in accounting policy are not the same as restatements from fraud.

Although investors think financial reporting follows strict rules, in actuality management has leeway in what rules to follow. (As shown in previous chapters, some actions are not necessarily illegal but are certainly aggressive.)

Disclosing Accounting Policies

Documents from the company contain many disclosures about accounting policies. MD&A must include information on what the SEC terms "critical accounting policies." Critical accounting policies are those that require estimates or judgments involving significant uncertainty.

For example, Hewlett-Packard's MD&A in the 2007 10-K informs the reader how it determines what is a critical policy:

> An accounting policy is deemed to be critical if it requires an accounting estimate to be made based on assumptions about matters that are highly uncertain at the time the estimate is made, if different estimates reasonably could have been used, or if changes in the estimate that are reasonably likely to occur could materially impact the financial statements. Management believes the following critical accounting policies reflect the significant estimates and assumptions used in the preparation of the Consolidated Financial Statements.

Then, Hewlett-Packard describes nine accounting policies that meet the definition of critical accounting policies. The descriptions point out the estimates and uncertainty associated with the policy.

For example, the description under the heading of "Allowance for Doubtful Accounts" from the 2007 10-K filing looks like this:

Allowance for Doubtful Accounts
We determine our allowance for doubtful accounts using a combination of factors to ensure that we have not overstated our trade and financing receivables balances due to uncollectibility. We maintain

an allowance for doubtful accounts for all customers based on a variety of factors, including the length of time receivables are past due, trends in overall weighted average risk rating of the total portfolio, macroeconomic conditions, significant one-time events, historical experience and the use of third-party credit risk models that generate quantitative measures of default probabilities based on market factors, and the financial condition of customers. Also, we record specific provisions for individual accounts when we become aware of a customer's inability to meet its financial obligations to us, such as in the case of bankruptcy filings or deterioration in the customer's operating results or financial position. If circumstances related to customers change, we would further adjust our estimates of the recoverability of receivables either upward or downward. The annual provision for doubtful accounts is approximately 0.03% of net revenue over the last three fiscal years. Using our third-party credit risk model at October 31, 2006, a 50-basis-point deterioration in either the weighted average default probabilities of our significant customers or in the overall mix of our portfolio would have resulted in an approximately $26 million increase to our trade allowance at the end of fiscal year 2006.

Note several things about this disclosure. First, it provides a reasonable amount of detail about how Hewlett-Packard estimates the amount of bad debts. Second, it shows the effect of conditions different from the estimate. In this case, if conditions are worse than those that informed the estimate, it would mean $26 million more than the estimate of bad debts.

MD&A is a rich source for information on accounting policies. The SEC has mandated that it provide information on critical accounting policies including what-if scenarios if estimates change.

Another source for the details of significant accounting policies is the first note included in the financial statements. Note 1 is always the disclosure of information about accounting policies used in the reports. Every company should report something on its revenue recognition policy. It's a good idea to compare the disclosure from one year to the next. Many large companies have their reports on the company website with a link to investor relations, so you don't have to store the paper copies if you have Internet service.

For example, compare Hewlett-Packard's disclosures from 2004, 2005, and 2006 relating to reclassifications and segment reorganization:

Reclassifications and Segment Reorganization (2004)

Certain reclassifications have been made to prior year amounts or balances in order to conform to the current year presentation. The long-term portion of deferred revenue previously classified as current deferred revenue has been reclassified to Other liabilities, and the prior year presentation also has been reclassified for comparative purposes. This reclassification did not impact HP's consolidated net revenue and also had no impact on HP's Consolidated Statements of Operations, Consolidated Statements of Cash Flows or Consolidated Statements of Stockholders' Equity for all periods presented. As further described in Note 18, at the beginning of the first quarter of fiscal 2004 HP's business segments were realigned. Prior period segment operating results have been restated for all periods presented to reflect the new organizational structure.

Reclassifications and Segment Reorganization (2005)

HP has made certain reclassifications to prior year amounts in order to conform to the current year presentation. In addition, HP reclassified certain information technology ("IT") infrastructure costs from selling, general and administrative expenses to cost of products, cost of services and research and development expenses to align the IT costs better with the functional areas they support. The impact of these reclassifications is an increase in cost of sales offset by an equal reduction of operating expenses, with no impact on consolidated or segment level earnings from operations.

HP has revised the presentation of its Consolidated Statements of Cash Flows for the fiscal year ended October 31, 2004 to reflect the gross purchases and sales of auction rate securities within cash flows from investing activities. This change does not affect previously reported subtotals within the Consolidated Statements of Cash Flows, or previously reported results of operations for any period presented.

Reclassifications and Segment Reorganization (2006)

HP has made certain organizational realignments in order to more closely align its financial reporting with its business structure. These realignments are immaterial in size and reflect primarily revenue shifts among business units within the same business segment. None of the changes impacts HP's previously reported consolidated net revenue, earnings from operations, net earnings or net earnings per share.

HP has revised the presentation of its Consolidated Statements of Cash Flows for the fiscal years ended October 31, 2005 and 2004 to provide improved visibility and comparability with the current year presentation. This change does not affect previously reported subtotals within the Consolidated Statements of Cash Flows, or previously reported results of operations for any period presented.

Looking at the disclosure over time gives readers a full picture of the reorganization activities undertaken by Hewlett-Packard. The 2005 note alerts readers to a jump in cost of sales and a decrease in operating expenses. Normal trend analysis would send up a red flag if the change was large, but the note explains why the trend is different.

Changing Accounting Methods

Companies change accounting methods regularly. The changes can be categorized as required or by choice. Required accounting changes occur when companies must apply new accounting standards. When the rules change, the company has no choice but to follow the new rules. For example, in December 2004, the FASB issued revised rules on accounting for stock options that require companies to record an expense for the options—something that few companies had been doing. The rule is effective for financial statements in 2005.

For example, in 2006, Hewlett-Packard explained the change in the notes:

Stock-Based Compensation

Effective November 1, 2005, HP adopted the fair value recognition provisions of SFAS No. 123 (revised 2004), "Share-Based Payment" ("SFAS 123R"), using the modified prospective transition method and therefore has not restated results for prior periods. Under this transition method, stock-based compensation expense in fiscal 2006 included stock-based compensation expense for all share-based payment awards granted prior to, but not yet vested as of November 1, 2005, based on the grant-date fair value estimated in accordance with the original provision of SFAS No. 123, "Accounting for Stock-Based Compensation" ("SFAS 123") . . ."

Hewlett-Packard and other companies were required to begin expensing stock options, a significant change in accounting method. Required accounting changes do not signal manipulation or fraud.

The other type of change may not be so benign. Managers can change the method of accounting to obscure performance problems. Three rules reduce the likelihood of investors being fooled. First, MD&A must reveal the impact of changes. Second, any prior-year financial statements included in the current-year report must be restated to show the results as if the new method had been used. Third, the notes to the financial statements must disclose changes in accounting policy.

New accounting rules require companies to restate any comparative information included with current financial reports. The term *restatement* may be misinterpreted. A company's stock price is punished if the restatement is due to fraud or errors, but the required adoption of a new accounting principle should not be a warning signal, even though the financials are restated. Investors need to carefully check the reason for the restatement to avoid missing an indicator of real problems or interpreting a legitimate, unavoidable restatement as a problem.

In many instances, management can choose one of several acceptable methods for measuring financial events. Using the same method over time allows investors to compare current performance to previous performance and make a meaningful evaluation of the improvement or decline. If the company changes the way it counts or measures, the change in performance may be manipulated and not the result of actual changes in business results. To help investors identify accounting changes, strict rules identify several forms of disclosure, including restatement of previous years' numbers. Investors need to determine the reason for the restatements to find problems in their portfolios.

CHAPTER 19

RELATED-PARTY TRANSACTION RUSE

AFTER DEFINING EXACTLY what constitutes related parties, we will identify the risks associated with related-party transactions and the disclosures required by accounting rules and SEC regulations.

What Are Related-Party Transactions?

A related-party transaction is any business deal that involves a subsidiary of the company, an employee, a director, a major

---

QUICK POINTS: RELATED-PARTY TRANSACTION RUSE

- ✧ Related-party transactions are between the company and a subsidiary, employee, director, or relative of one of those people.
- ✧ Disclosure requirements are as follows:
  - ✧ Accounting rules require disclosure of related-party transactions in the notes to the financial statements.
  - ✧ SEC regulations require disclosure of related-party transactions, and companies often do this in proxy statements.
- ✧ Related-party transactions may represent the background of a corporation as a family business that was successful.
- ✧ Measurement amounts may not reflect shareholders' interests.
- ✧ Unnecessary expenditures are really disguised compensation to directors or executives.
- ✧ Related-party transactions can disguise bribes to directors.
- ✧ Frivolous expenditures may be disguised as customary.

---

investor, or a close relative of an employee, director, or major investor. Related-party transactions are common enough that both the SEC and the FASB have made rules about how companies must reveal related-party transactions.

What Are the Disclosure Requirements Regarding Related-Party Transactions?

That's the great thing about accounting and SEC rules. The information is right in the annual report and proxy statements. Related-party transactions must be disclosed in the notes to the financial statements according to the accounting rules. The proxy statements sent to investors before the annual meeting usually inform shareholders about related-party transactions and satisfy SEC regulations. In addition, good corporate governance includes some kind of authorization of related-party transactions by the board of directors or the audit committee. Those actions should be included in the minutes of the meetings of those bodies.

Not All Related-Party Transactions Are Bad

Related-party transactions may be a good thing. Working with relatives or others who have a deep stake in the company may produce better results than working with outsiders. Homeowners planning a big home improvement project would probably choose a contractor they knew over an unknown. The Gap revealed in its 2005 annual report that FDI, one of the contractors that constructs and remodels stores, is owned by the brother of the company founder. That related-party transaction resulted in payments of $21 million to FDI during 2005. If the bidding is competitive and the process fair, you could argue that this related-party transaction was a better value because FDI would be more attentive and careful in work for a relative.

Related-party transactions may also exist because the corporation has its roots in a family business that became very successful. Before condemning all related-party transactions, it is important to investigate them, being aware of some of the problems associated with them.

Ruse #1: Measurement Amounts May Not Reflect Shareholders' Interests

In normal business transactions, the parties are acting in their own self-interest, but in related-party transactions that may not be the case. Take the purchase of a used vehicle, for example. The dealer is trying to sell the car for the highest price possible and still make the sale. The buyer is trying to buy the car for the lowest price possible and still buy the car. The tension between the parties produces a neutral result that doesn't favor one party or the other. Change the parties involved to a parent and child, and, in the normal harmonious family, the tension of trying to sell for the greatest price and buy at the lowest price isn't present. The parent may want to help the child and agree to a price that is lower than an outsider would pay. Or the child may want to use the transaction to subsidize an aging parent's income and be willing to pay a higher price than the market value. When the parties to a transaction are related, the value measurements are not reliable.

Related-person transactions are troublesome, but if the related party is another business entity that is somehow associated with the company, the problems may be more pervasive. Not only do investors wonder about waste or the lack of fairness that are a risk of related-party transactions, but measurement problems make evaluating the performance of an investment difficult. Revenues from sales with related parties might be recorded at prices that are higher than arm's-length transactions if the company wants to prop up the related party. Or those revenues could be below market value to benefit the company. Assessing sales revenue is difficult when the parties are related.

Ruse #2: Unnecessary Expenditures Are Really Disguised Compensation to Directors or Executives

In addition to measurement issues, related-party transactions may be unnecessary transactions whose only function is to supplement the compensation of employees, directors, major investors, or other connected people. One common related-party transaction is for the company to pay for the use of a plane owned by one of the executives. Corporations like Nike, Apple, Gateway, and Time Warner have all had executives that owned planes and were paid for their use. Stockholders should question whether this is really necessary to save travel time and money or if it is a form of hidden compensation.

Ruse #3: Related-Party Transactions Can Disguise Bribes to Directors

Transactions with insiders may be a way of bribing them. Using consulting services from a member of the board of directors could be a sneaky way to keep the director from being critical of company management. Employing a director's or executive's spouse or child might be a way to gain the goodwill and cooperation of that insider.

Ruse #4: Frivolous or Extravagant Expenditures Can Be Made to Seem Typical or Standard

All related-party transactions need careful inspection. Just because the company discloses the transaction doesn't necessarily mean it is sensible.

For example, Pilgrim's Pride discloses quite a few related-party transactions on its website (www.pilgrimspride.com/investors/relatedpartytransactions.aspx). There it states that Pilgrim's Pride rents egg production facilities from the CEO of the company, Lonnie "Bo" Pilgrim, for $62,500 a month and goes on to say that "management believes that the terms of this agreement . . . are substantially similar to, and contain terms not less favorable to us than, agreements obtainable from unaffiliated parties." The company also buys chickens from Mr. Pilgrim, leases an airplane from him, maintains deposits in banks in which Mr. Pilgrim is a major stockholder, pays something called an "affiliate" of Mr. Pilgrim $1.6 million for guaranteeing company debt, plus it employs three of Mr. Pilgrim's children, each with a salary over $200,000. All of these transactions are explained as either being approved by the Audit Committee or "substantially the same as contracts entered into by the Company with unaffiliated parties." The disturbing signal in this example is the number and variety of transactions associated with the CEO.

Another example that is disclosed in the proxy statement is in the Aaron Rents notice of the annual meeting of shareholders in 2006. Aaron Rents, Inc., is a furniture rental company based in Atlanta. In the section on related-party transactions, this company claims that as part of its marketing program, it sponsors a professional NASCAR driver. That doesn't seem so bad, but that driver implemented a NASCAR driver development program and the two sons of the company president were in that program at a cost of nearly $1 million in 2006. That sounds like the company is paying for the president's kids to play race car driver. The marketing program is spelled out, but following the thread to the driver development program is confusing. The disclosure tries to make it seem as though all the NASCAR activities are really part of the marketing program. The red flag here is the weak tie between marketing and the driver development program.

Related-party transactions may simply reflect the structure of the original family business, but in a corporate environment related-party transactions provide the opportunity for abuse. The chance for insiders to benefit themselves rather than act in the best interests of shareholders means that investors must scrutinize the disclosures regarding this type of transaction. Careful reading will help investors identify the transactions that are based on a higher level of trust for family and those transactions that are tricks to enrich employees and directors.

CHAPTER 20

CONTINGENCY CAPER

WE NOW LOOK at an interesting aspect of financial reports: the monetary effects of events that *might* happen. When assessing whether to keep, sell, or buy stock in a particular company, investors should know about contingencies—things that might happen in the future and the financial effect of those occurrences. Contingencies are another aspect of a company's financial reporting that involves flexibility and judgment. And as we have seen before, when flexible accounting rules give management the opportunity to choose how to report an event, the choice is almost always the most favorable treatment.

QUICK POINTS: CONTINGENCY CAPER

✦ Contingencies are events that have not happened but will have financial consequences for the company if they do.
✦ Only contingent losses are considered worthy of reporting.
✦ Contingencies are either ignored, disclosed in the notes, or recorded as an estimated loss.
✦ The company sets up a reserve to cover the loss if the event is likely to happen and the company can estimate the amount of the loss.
✦ When the event finally happens, the reserve is reversed.
✦ Cookie jar reserves result if estimates of the loss are higher than the actual loss, because the leftover reserve amount increases income.
✦ Reviewing a company's contingencies over time can reveal earnings manipulation.

The Basics of Contingencies

In addition to historical reporting on what happened during the recently completed accounting period, companies must also consider contingencies before issuing their financial statements. A contingency is an event that has not yet happened, but may. If the event does happen, it will have financial consequences for the company. Lawsuits or environmental problems are common examples of situations that could cause a company to record a contingency.

Reporting contingencies is lopsided. Only losses are considered. That means a company can't record anything for the huge contract in the final stages of negotiation that will add 10 percent to revenue or for the patent infringement lawsuit that is close to awarding the company between $500,000 and $1 million in damages. Both of those would be gains, or increases in income, and the contingency rules do not allow recording anything about contingent gains in the formal financial statements. Management can mention them in the discussion in the annual report but not show the increases on the income statement . . . at least not until the sales from the contract happen or the lawsuit's award is final.

Management, with input from attorneys and accountants, assesses contingencies at the end of the accounting period. At that time, they identify the contingencies and determine the likelihood of occurrence. Any contingency that has a remote possibility of happening is ignored. The logic is that it will only confuse the readers to include things that are extremely unlikely to happen. Imagine reading in every financial report about contingencies for flood, lightning strikes, and other remote risks. It would obscure the serious contingencies.

After eliminating the remote contingencies, managers, with professional help from attorneys and accountants, try to estimate the amount of the loss that could result from each of the remaining contingencies and the likelihood that each one will happen. At that point, two methods of accounting for the contingencies are available to the managers. The first is to disclose the contingency in the notes to the financial statements. This method is used for events with a possibility of happening but that are not probable. It is also used for losses that can't be estimated. The second method is to reduce income by the amount of the estimate and establish a reserve, or a liability, on the balance. The reserve is then reduced when the event happens. The second method is used if the occurrence of the contingency is judged to be probable.

The two methods have very different effects on the income statement. The first method—disclosure only—does not decrease income, and the second method—taking the loss and setting up a reserve—does. When contingent losses are recorded, the decrease in income occurs even before the event actually happens.

Caper #1: Assess Likelihood Most Favorably

The assessment of likelihood of occurrence is not a science. The accounting rules don't give precise probabilities for what is considered a remote chance of occurrence, a possible chance of occurrence, or a probable chance of occurrence. This means that company management can use the flexibility in the accounting rules to advantage. They analyze the situation to categorize the event based on likelihood of happening.

This caper, however, is not easy to pull off. Although the weather events are considered remote, almost any lawsuit that is under way is disclosed because it is usually possible that there will be a loss. It would be very risky, if not foolhardy, to not disclose existing lawsuits.

In the 2006 Procter & Gamble annual report, on page 61, the following statement covers those contingencies relating to lawsuits:

> We are subject to various lawsuits and claims with respect to matters such as governmental regulations, income taxes and other actions arising out of the normal course of business. While considerable

uncertainty exists, in the opinion of management and our counsel, the ultimate resolution of the various lawsuits and claims will not materially affect our financial condition, cash flows or results of operations. We are also subject to contingencies pursuant to environmental laws and regulations that in the future may require us to take action to correct the effects on the environment of prior manufacturing and waste disposal practices. Based on currently available information, we do not believe the ultimate resolution of environmental remediation will have a material adverse effect on our financial position, cash flows or results of operations.

Caper #2: Estimate Loss Low

In addition to estimating the likelihood of occurrence, company management must also estimate the amount of a contingent loss. For contingencies that are probable, this estimate is important because it becomes the amount of the decrease in income. The motivation may be to minimize the decrease in the current period income to meet earnings expectations or bonus thresholds. In that case, managers could make a low estimate of the loss, resulting in a smaller decrease in income than if a generous estimate was made.

The consequence of this low estimate is that a future income will be lower if the actual loss is greater than the low estimate. But company management figures that the time lag will give them the opportunity to make it up. Then readers of the financial statements will never notice that the estimate was too low.

Perhaps the ultimate low estimate is being unable to make any estimate of the loss. The estimation task can be difficult, but, remember, even for likely contingencies, if no estimate is possible, then income is not reduced.

For example, an interesting situation arose in 2004 at Merck, with the voluntary withdrawal of the painkiller Vioxx. The notes to the 2004 financial statements disclosed the lawsuits but record a reserve only for the legal defense costs, not for the actual costs of losing a lawsuit:

Reserves

The Company currently anticipates that one or more of the *Vioxx* Product Liability Lawsuits may go to trial in the first half of 2005. The Company cannot predict the timing of any trials with respect to the *Vioxx* Shareholder Lawsuits. The Company believes that it has meritorious defenses to the *Vioxx* Lawsuits and will vigorously defend against them. In view of the inherent difficulty of predicting the outcome of litigation, particularly where there are many claimants and the claimants seek indeterminate damages, the Company is unable to predict the outcome of these matters, and at this time cannot reasonably estimate the possible loss or range of loss with respect to the *Vioxx* Lawsuits. The Company has not established any reserves for any potential liability relating to the *Vioxx* Lawsuits or the *Vioxx* Investigations (collectively the "*Vioxx* Litigation"). The Company has established a reserve of $675 million solely for its future legal defense costs related to the *Vioxx* Litigation. This reserve is based on certain assumptions and is the minimum amount that the Company believes at this time it can reasonably estimate will be spent over a multi-year period. The Company significantly increased the reserve when it had the ability to reasonably estimate its future legal defense costs for the *Vioxx* Litigation.

Caper #3: Estimate Loss High

In some cases, companies book high estimates of contingent losses. While that reduces income in the current period, it provides management with a cushion that can be released at a later date. As time passes, the estimate of the loss for the contingency becomes clearer, and management can reduce the reserve, which increases income. This reversal of the reserve can come at an opportunistic time to rescue a period of weak earnings.

Detection Techniques

Detecting bad reserve estimates prior to the outcome is difficult for several reasons. First, the disclosure is not clear and situated consistently in the annual report. The easiest way to find the information is to search a PDF format annual report for "contingency" and "reserve." The most effective analysis is to compare the notes over time.

Comparing Merck's disclosures about Vioxx in 2002 to the 2005 disclosures gives readers a clear picture of the importance of the situation. In 2002 the disclosure was short and simple:

> A number of federal and state lawsuits, involving individual claims as well as purported class actions, have been filed against the Company with respect to Vioxx. Some of the lawsuits also name as defendants Pfizer Inc. and Pharmacia, which market a competing product. The lawsuits include allegations regarding gastrointestinal bleeding and cardiovascular events. The Company believes that these lawsuits are completely without merit and will vigorously defend against them.

Then in 2003 a little more discussion is presented:

> Federal and state lawsuits involving numerous individual claims, as well as some putative class actions, have been filed against the Company with respect to Vioxx. Some of the lawsuits also name as a defendant Pfizer Inc., which markets a competing product. Certain of the lawsuits include allegations regarding gastrointestinal bleeding, cardiovascular events and kidney damage. The lawsuits have been filed in federal courts as well as in a number of state courts. While cases in other jurisdictions are proceeding separately, the actions filed in the state courts of California and New Jersey have been transferred to a single judge in each state for coordinated proceedings. The Company anticipates that one or more of the lawsuits in various jurisdictions may go to trial in the first half of 2004. Litigation is inherently subject to uncertainties and no assurance can be given on the outcome of any given trial. However, the Company

believes that these lawsuits are without merit and will vigorously defend against them.

In 2005, Merck still does not record a reserve for anything other than the cost of defense:

> . . . The Company will continue to monitor its legal defense costs and review the adequacy of the associated reserves. The Company currently anticipates that a number of Vioxx Product Liability Lawsuits will be tried in 2006. The Company cannot predict the timing of any trials with respect to the Vioxx Shareholder Lawsuits. The Company believes that it has meritorious defenses to the Vioxx Lawsuits and will vigorously defend against them. In view of the inherent difficulty of predicting the outcome of litigation, particularly where there are many claimants and the claimants seek indeterminate damages, the Company is unable to predict the outcome of these matters, and at this time cannot reasonably estimate the possible loss or range of loss with respect to the Vioxx Lawsuits. The Company has not established any reserves for any potential liability relating to the Vioxx Litigation.

However, the Vioxx situation is discussed extensively in various parts of the annual report. A search of the PDF document yields over 100 references to Vioxx.

Contingencies are an unusual part of financial reporting because the amounts, if any, are speculative. Contingency information is useful for investors to spot things that might affect future results. Usually these possible events aren't known to outsiders. Without required reporting, investors would be unaware of the possibility of future negative effects on the company's performance.

PART VI

EVALUATING THE EVIDENCE IN THE ANNUAL REPORT AND SEC FILINGS

CASH FROM OPERATIONS CONS

THE STATEMENT OF Cash Flows is a relatively new financial statement (just a little over two decades old). It replaced an obtuse statement that was supposed to explain the changes in financial position but was hopeless because it wasn't always based on cash. Now there is a statement to explain the change in cash from one period to the next.

Statement of Cash Flows

The Statement of Cash Flows classifies cash flows according to three sources. The first source of cash is from operating activi-

---

QUICK POINTS: CASH FROM OPERATIONS CONS

- The Statement of Cash Flows classifies cash flows as relating to operating, financing, or investing activities.
- Companies can boost cash flow from operations by slowing down payments to suppliers or by financing payables.
- Companies can manipulate cash flow from operations by securitizing receivables or by factoring them.
- Companies can misclassify cash flows to present a stronger cash picture.
- Ratios using cash from operations can give a clear picture of a company's financial health.
- Careful reading of the notes accompanying the financial statements can alert readers to companies that are using cash from operations cons.

---

ties. The section on the cash flows associated with operating activities is presented either directly, with items such as cash from customers, cash paid to employees, cash paid for inventory, and cash paid for taxes, or indirectly. The indirect method starts with net income and adjusts it for all the noncash items such as depreciation, amortization, uncollected sales, and unpaid expenses of the period. Either way, the cash from operating activities will end up being the same dollar amount and represents the cash the company generates internally from sales.

Cash from operating activities is rarely equal to net income because net income is based on accrual accounting. Net income includes sales for which the company has not been paid, so sales revenue is often larger than the amount in cash received from customers. Net income also includes noncash expenses like depreciation, warranty expense, and bad debt expense, resulting in higher expenses than the cash paid for expenses.

The second source of cash flows is from investing activities. The most common investing activities include things like capital expenditures for property, plant, and equipment. Other investing activities involve selling noncurrent assets, making loans, and being repaid. Usually cash flows from investing activities are negative because of the purchase of noncurrent assets for use in the business. If a company has a large positive cash flow from investing activities over time, it could be selling off assets to sustain cash. That is a warning signal because eventually the company will have no assets left to sell or use in the business.

The third source of cash flows is from financing activities. Financing activities include borrowing and repaying loans, selling stock, and paying dividends. New SEC rules require a company to include the tax benefits it receives when employees exercise their stock options in this section. This new rule is a change from the previous classification of the tax benefit from stock option exercise as an operating activity cash flow. The new rule will result in lower cash from operating activities and higher cash from financing activities.

The Statement of Cash Flows is considered more pristine and less contrived than the other financial statements because it is based on cash. However, companies can engage in some activities that cloud the clear picture.

Con #1: Boosting Cash Flow with Payables

One way to increase cash flows from operating activities is to slow down the payment of accounts payable. Companies lengthen the time it takes to pay a bill, insisting it is good cash management. An increase in the amount of accounts payable over the year is added to net income to get cash from operating activities, using the indirect method. An increase in the amount of accounts payable reduces the cash paid for expenses, thereby increasing cash from operating activities using the direct method.

The delay of payment to creditors, though, can have negative effects. First, suppliers may be reluctant to sell to a company that is slow to pay or may increase prices to make up for the delay in receiving cash. Second, the delay causes a one-time increase, making it hard to sustain the new level of cash from operating activities.

An alternative to slow payment is a financing technique using payables. The company arranges for a bank to pay the suppliers on time, thus preserving the company's credit standing. The company agrees to repay the bank at some time in the future the amount plus a service charge. This technique seems just like a short-term loan. The problem is that normally the cash paid to suppliers is a cash outflow in the operating activities section. When this technique is used, the company classifies the payment as a financing activity. Companies that do this can determine the optimum amount to shift to financing so as to preserve a desirable level of cash flow from operating activities.

Con #2: Manipulating Cash Flow with Receivables

Securitizations can increase cash flow from operating activities over the short run. In a securitization, a company collects a large number of its receivables and transfers them to a bank or a variable-interest entity. The company receives cash for the transfer. Oftentimes the company continues to service the receivables, and when the payments on the receivables arrive, the company uses the proceeds to make payments to the bank or variable-interest entity to which the receivables were transferred. If done properly, the company can recognize the cash received from the securitization as a cash inflow from operating activities.

Securitizations can involve two problems. The first is that a securitization produces an increase in cash flow that is hard to sustain because securitization is expensive and complicated, limiting the amount of times the company can do it. Second, in some cases because of measurement of long-term receivables, the company might record a gain on the sale of the receivables. Neither accounting rules nor SEC rules specify where the gain should go. Some companies aggressively include such gains in revenue.

Factoring is another way for a company to receive cash immediately for its receivables. Factoring usually involves the sale of short-term receivables rather than long-term and results in the company receiving less than the face amount of the receivables.

Con #3: Misclassifying Cash Flows

Companies are motivated to increase cash from operating activities if at all possible. To do so, sometimes a company will misclassify an item. One example is the gain on the sale of trading securities. While normally the sale of investments is considered an investing activity, if the investment is in the trading securities category, the cash received may be included in the operating activities section. This is the same for any borrowing to conduct purchases of trading securities. These investment activities are not part of the usual business operations and as such are misclassified when included in cash flows from operating activities.

Another misclassification problem has come about because of a recent SEC ruling. The tax benefits of stock option exercise were in the operating activities section prior to 2007. These tax benefits occur when employees exercise options, and the difference between the strike price and the market price is a tax deduction to the company. Now those benefits must be part of financing activities, resulting in significant decrease in cash from operations for tech companies that use options extensively. Companies also use cash to buy back shares of stock in the market when employees exercise their options. The company is trying to avoid a serious reduction in earnings per share. The cash used to buy back shares is a financing outflow. The classification of the tax benefits and buyback dollars as financing activities seems incorrect. Stock options are really a form of compensation. Paying employees is an operating activity. These two cash flows arise from the exercise of options and should be considered operating activities.

Although the Statement of Cash Flows is harder to manipulate, it is still possible for companies to con readers into thinking the cash flow situation is better than it is. Investors can use ratio analysis and careful reading of the filings to find these cons.

Detection Technique: Ratios

Cash flow ratios can help you analyze your investments and spot problems. The first useful calculation is free cash flow. Free cash flow is equal to cash from operating activities less capital expenditures. Both of these numbers can be found in the SEC filings. Free cash flow is the cash that remains at the end of the accounting period after paying all the normal bills of the business, including taxes, and after the capital expenditures made to maintain or expand the business. This is the cash available for dividends or share buybacks.

Another useful ratio is net income to cash from operating activities. Dividing net income by cash from operating activities should result in a ratio close to 1. If the ratio is significantly larger, it could mean that the company is not generating cash from normal business activities but from peripheral ones, like the sale of assets.

The operating cash flow ratio is equal to cash from operating activities divided by current liabilities. This ratio helps investors evaluate whether the company is generating enough cash for its current bills. A ratio below 1 means the company is not creating the necessary cash to meet current liabilities, suggesting that the company will have to slow payments or borrow to meet its short-term obligations. Borrowing is difficult if you can't pay your current bills. But beyond that basic interpretation, this ratio is useful only if compared to an industry average or to that of another company in the same industry because it varies greatly, depending on the industry.

The next ratio reveals how easily the company can manage its debt. The cash to current debt coverage ratio is calculated using cash from operating activities minus the cash dividends in the numerator. The denominator is equal to current liabilities that are interest bearing. Examples of items found on the balance sheet that usually are interest bearing include short-term debt, short-term borrowings, current portion of long-term debt, and debt maturing within a year. Non-interest-bearing current liabilities include accounts payable, deferred or un-earned revenue, taxes payable, deferred tax liabilities, accrued liabilities, and other current liabilities. This ratio shows the effect of dividend payment on the company's ability to comfortably carry its debt load. A higher ratio means it is easier for the company to handle the debt.

In addition to looking at the ratios compared to those of other companies in the same industry or in comparison to industry averages, trend analysis is a key tool for spotting problems in cash flow. The ratios should remain stable, and any significant changes could indicate problems. Comparing the trend in cash from operating activities to the trend in net income is another useful analysis for spotting trouble.

Detection Technique: Notes

The disclosures in the notes and in MD&A are valuable sources of information about cash flow. An important disclosure relates to the classification of a gain from sale of trading securities. As discussed, a company can misclassify items on the Statement of Cash Flows. The following is from General Motors' 2004 annual report and reveals a previous misclassification.

Statements of Cash Flows

After considering the concerns raised by the staff of the SEC, management has concluded that certain prior year balances in the Consolidated Statements of Cash Flows should be reclassified to appropriately present net cash provided by operating activities and net cash used in investing activities.

The Corporation's previous policy was to classify all the cash flow effects of providing wholesale loans to its independent dealers by GM's Financing and Insurance Operations as an investing activity in its Consolidated Statements of Cash Flows. This policy, when applied to the financing of inventory sales, had the effect of presenting an investing cash outflow and an operating cash inflow even though there was no cash inflow or outflow on a consolidated basis. The Corporation has changed its policy to eliminate this intersegment activity from its Consolidated Statements of Cash Flows and, as a result of this change, all cash flow effects related to wholesale loans are reflected in the operating activities section of the Consolidated Statement of Cash Flows for 2004. This reclassification better reflects the financing of the sale of inventory as a non-cash transaction to GM on a consolidated basis and eliminates the effects of intercompany transactions.

The notes also reveal exactly what the company includes in cash and cash equivalents. Note 1 in the 2004 IBM annual report, available on the company website, lists a cash equivalent heading, which contains the following information:

> All highly liquid investments with maturities of three months or less at the date of purchase are carried at fair value and considered to be cash equivalents.

This same wording is found in many corporate reports and is not particularly revealing.

The Statement of Cash Flows provides useful information to investors about the reasons for the change in the cash during the year. It does this by separating out the sources and uses of cash into three categories: operating activities, investing activities, and financing activities. Although the Statement of Cash Flows is less susceptible to manipulation than the income statement and balance sheet, companies can still con investors by boosting cash flow with techniques involving the slow payment or financing of payables. Companies also manipulate cash flow through securitization or factoring of receivables. In addition, companies can misclassify cash flows to mislead investors.

CHAPTER 22

MANAGEMENT DISCUSSION AND ANALYSIS

SEC REGULATIONS REQUIRE management to discuss and analyze certain aspects of the company. Recent SEC guidance and actions have emphasized the importance of management discussion and analysis (MD&A) as an information source for increasing users' understanding of the financial statements. If management is honest and open in the MD&A, it lends support to the conclusion that overall management is honest.

QUICK POINTS: MANAGEMENT DISCUSSION AND ANALYSIS

- ✧ According to the SEC, the purpose of MD&A is
  - ✧ To help investors "see the company through the eyes of management."
  - ✧ To "provide the context" for user analysis.
  - ✧ To provide not only the numbers representing earnings and cash flow but also information about the likelihood that those numbers will continue, allowing users to predict future performance.
- ✧ Requirements include:
  - ✧ Format.
  - ✧ Facts.
- ✧ Look for the following:
  - ✧ Clarity.
  - ✧ That the business description matches the MD&A.
  - ✧ Comparison to the previous year.
  - ✧ Openness.

What Is MD&A?

The purpose of MD&A is to give readers of the financial statements one more aid in understanding those statements. The SEC's objective for MD&A is to help investors understand the company the way management does. That understanding provides a context for analyzing the financial statements. Additionally, MD&A should help investors predict future performance because it reports on the quality and variability of the items in the financial statements.

In December 2003, the SEC issued guidance on MD&A that emphasizes the format and characteristics of the narrative as much as the required content. The SEC gives tips on organizing and presenting MD&A in a way that enhances readability and understanding. It recommends a good overview that includes relevant economic factors, industry factors, a discussion of business activities, and a description of the trends that management is focused on. The entire MD&A should present only material information and not overwhelm the reader with too many details. The SEC admonishes companies to avoid using boilerplate MD&A.

The SEC requires certain disclosures in MD&A, one of which regards liquidity and debt. The discussion must include substantive information on cash flows including uncertainties and future cash requirements. The SEC warns companies that a restatement of items on the Statement of Cash Flows is not sufficient to satisfy this requirement.

Another required disclosure is information on critical accounting estimates. The SEC requires companies to provide information on the effect of changing the estimates or the effect of one estimate versus another. This disclosure is required only if the change or effect makes a material difference in the financial condition or operating performance. An example of such a disclosure is a possible change in the rate estimates used in pension accounting. The estimate of the rate of return on pension assets affects the amount of pension expense per period and the amount of reported additional pension liability. To satisfy SEC requirements for critical accounting estimates, the company should compute the effect of a possible rate change and disclose it if the effect is material. In 2002 GE had a $5 billion loss in its pension fund that it disclosed in the footnotes, but there was no mention of it in the MD&A.

After the Enron scandal revealed many off-balance-sheet entities that served to hide debt and other obligations from readers of the financial statements, the Sarbanes-Oxley Act was passed and included a provision relating to disclosure of these special-purpose entities. Companies must disclose all material off-balance-sheet transactions in a separate section of MD&A. Companies involved in things like guarantee contracts, contingent interests in assets owned or transferred to another entity, derivatives classified as equity, or variable interests in other entities must assess the effect of those arrangements on the company's position and performance. If the effect could be material, the company must disclose enough information so that readers can understand the purpose, importance, and risks associated with the off-balance-sheet items.

One of the objectives for MD&A—helping investors predict future performance with information on variability and sustainability of current performance—requires discussion of trends that affect the company. Companies are reluctant to be too forthcoming because the trends usually indicate problems. That reluctance can result in real problems for executives who are not completely open, as Kmart executives found when the SEC filed a civil complaint for misleading investors about reasons for financial problems at the company prior to the bankruptcy. The former CEO and CFO misled investors in matters relating to inventory and the company's liquidity. They are awaiting trial at this time. In contrast, Berkshire Hathaway has been known to include very informative information in its MD&A.

What Are the Signals to Watch in MD&A?

The first signal is the writing style. It should be clear and easy to understand. An overview or introduction and headings should help readers comprehend the important aspects of the discussion. The writing should not be a rehash of numbers available in the financial statements. Instead, it should identify changes, causes, and trends.

The second signal is verifying that the information in the MD&A is consistent with the information in the financial statements. A company that has a heavy debt load on the balance sheet should discuss that debt in the liquidity section of the MD&A. A company with declining revenues over the last period should discuss the reason for that decline in the MD&A.

The third signal is boilerplate prose. Compare the current MD&A to that of the last period. It should be different. The MD&A should not be prepared from a template, by just changing numbers. That won't identify trends and changes in the business environment.

The final signal is a subtle one and relies on instinct. Ask yourself if the MD&A really aids in your understanding of the company and its operations. If you answer yes, it suggests that management is open and honest in other business activities, too. If you answer no, then management may be hiding things from investors.

CHAPTER 23

INTERNAL CONTROL

THE SARBANES-OXLEY ACT of 2002 has changed many things in the business world, but perhaps the most controversial has to do with internal control. Internal control has always been important to auditors who used an assessment of the company's internal control system to plan the audit. The better the control system, the less detail work was needed. Now, however, both management and the auditors must specifically report on the effectiveness of a part of the internal control system—the part that controls financial reporting. This is a good thing for investors because it is zeroing in on the controls that should deter fraudulent financial reporting. The hope is partly that investors will feel more

---

QUICK POINTS: INTERNAL CONTROL

✧ Internal control is the system of practices and procedures inside a company to ensure that business activities are performed in a manner that is honest and good for the company.
✧ The Sarbanes-Oxley Act requires two reports on internal control over part of the company's internal control system, the internal control over financial reporting.
✧ Problems with the internal control system can include:
  ✧ A control deficiency.
  ✧ A significant deficiency.
  ✧ A material weakness.
✧ Investors can find the two reports in SEC filings.

---

confident about the financial reports and will invest freely. Although restoring investor confidence is necessary, not everyone is sure that the benefits are worth the cost of the new requirements.

What Is Internal Control?

Internal control is defined by the Committee of Sponsoring Organizations as "a process, effected by an entity's board of directors, management, and other personnel, designed to provide reasonable assurance regarding the achievement of objectives in the following categories—effectiveness and efficiency of operations, reliability of financial reporting, and compliance with applicable laws and regulations." Boiling that down to the essence of internal control, you could say that internal control is a system of practices and procedures within the company that ensure the business activities are performed honestly and in a way that is good for the company. Internal control is necessary because the owners, shareholders, aren't on-site to supervise to make sure that employees aren't stealing or acting in a way that is detrimental to the business.

For example, in a large business, bills are paid only if a purchase order documenting the order, an invoice documenting the charge, and a receiving report documenting the receipt of the items are attached. Then the clerk can prepare a check, confident that the order was legitimate and the items were received.

Internal control has always been important, but new rules expand the importance to a broader group of people. Auditors have relied on the internal control system in a company to reduce the amount of procedures performed, rewarding the company that possesses good internal control with lower audit fees. Owners have relied on the internal control system to control employee actions. But with the passage of the Sarbanes-Oxley Act in 2002, a new emphasis on a part of internal control has emerged that serves investors.

What Part Did Sarbanes-Oxley Play in the Increased Importance of Internal Control?

The Sarbanes-Oxley Act was passed in reaction to corporate scandals. In each business meltdown, the financial reports hadn't seemed to convey information that investors could have used to discern the problems, even though auditors attested to the fairness of those reports. The system of controls didn't work, and the audit didn't protect investors from fraud. In addition to many other provisions, Sarbanes-Oxley requires both management and auditors to report on internal control over financial reporting. In addition, the auditors also report on management's report.

Management must report on internal control over financial reporting at least annually. The report focuses on three things. First, management should review the processes in place to promote accuracy in the company's accounting records. Second, management should assess the procedures used to prepare the financial statements and notes that are for external users, like investors. This aspect should emphasize that revenues and expenditures are appropriately recognized. The third focus is to scrutinize the system that is supposed to prevent or detect material fraud in the financial statements.

The report by management must be very direct. It must indicate that either internal control over financial reporting is effective or it is ineffective. The report can't just say that nothing bad was found, but must explicitly state effective or ineffective. Also, the report can't imply that part of the system is effective. For example, it couldn't say internal control over financial reporting is effective except for the controls dealing with stock options. The report can't say that part of the internal control over financial reporting is fine but another part isn't. Management's report must be clear and unequivocal that the system of internal control over financial reporting is effective or ineffective.

In addition to management's report, the auditors must issue two reports on internal control over financial reporting. The first is an assessment of management's report. The second is the auditors' assessment of internal control over financial reporting. The auditors can issue an unqualified opinion on management's report that identifies problems but an adverse opinion on the internal control over financial reporting if problems in that area exist. These two auditor opinions are in addition to the opinion on the whole of the financial statements. Auditors can issue an unqualified opinion even if there are problems with internal control over financial reporting. The auditors will just have to do more procedures to satisfy themselves that the statements are fair.

What Kinds of Problems Might Management Find?

No internal control system is perfect and able to completely eliminate the possibility of fraud. Internal control systems are supposed to provide reasonable assurance that things are being done properly. Internal control over financial reporting should be designed to provide this assurance. Two types of flaws in the internal control system can cause problems. The first is a design flaw. A design flaw means that some control is missing. The internal control system is operating properly, but because of the way it is designed, the system won't prevent or detect misstatements. The second flaw is an operating flaw, meaning that although a control is in place, it isn't working to prevent or detect misstatements. The seriousness of these problems determines whether internal control over financial reporting is effective or not.

The Public Company Accounting Oversight Board has defined three levels of deficiencies, or problems, with internal control over financial reporting. A *control deficiency* is the least serious; it is simply a control whose design or operation doesn't prevent or detect misstatements on a timely basis. A *significant deficiency* is the next level of seriousness; it is a control deficiency or a collection of control deficiencies that could allow a small misstatement to exist undetected. A *material weakness* is a significant deficiency or collection of significant deficiencies that could allow a material misstatement to exist undetected. The three-tier system relies on the likelihood of the deficient control allowing a misstatement and the materiality of the misstatement.

If a company identifies a material weakness, it is a big problem. In January 2007, Broadcom filed an amended Form 10-K for 2005 with this disclosure:

Management's Report on Internal Control over Financial Reporting

Our management is responsible for establishing and maintaining adequate internal control over financial reporting, as such term is defined in Exchange Act Rule 13a-15(f). Under the supervision and with the participation of our management, including our principal executive officer and principal financial officer, we conducted an evaluation of the effectiveness of our internal control over financial reporting based on the framework set forth in Internal Control—Integrated Framework issued by the Committee of Sponsoring Organizations of the Treadway Commission. Based on our evaluation under the framework set forth in Internal Control—Integrated Framework, our management, in assessing the findings of the voluntary review as well as the restatement of our financial statements in the context of paragraph 139 of AS 2, concluded that internal control over financial reporting was not effective as of December 31, 2005 because there was a material weakness with respect to our former chief financial officer's role in the application of accounting principles as it pertains to certain equity awards granted prior to June 2003, including the impact on the 2005 financial statements of amortizing deferred compensation related to those equity awards. Management's assessment of the effectiveness of our internal control over financial reporting as of December 31, 2005 has been audited by Ernst & Young LLP, our independent registered public accounting firm, as stated in its report which is included herewith.

The auditors also reported on the amended 10-K, saying that they revised their opinion and management did not maintain effective internal control over financial reporting in 2005.

Essentially, Broadcom got caught in the stock options backdating scandal and had to revise its report on internal control over financial reporting for a previous year. Interestingly, it didn't seem to affect the 2006 10-K that provided this disclosure regarding internal control over financial reporting because management assessed internal control over financial reporting as effective in 2006.

It is interesting to see how the auditors reacted to the situation. In 2005, both management and the auditors issued reports indicating that internal control over financial reporting was effective. Both missed the material weakness that allowed backdating of stock options. What would be the effect on the auditor's opinion on management's report for 2006? Apparently the problem with internal control over financial reporting is solved because both management's and the auditor's reports indicate that it is effective.

Where Do You Find the Information on Internal Control?

The SEC allows the public to use the filing database for no charge. The first step is to log on to the SEC website at www.sec.gov. Next, click on Filings and Forms (EDGAR). Then find the Central Index Key (CIK) for your company, a feature on the Filings and Forms page. An investor can find the number associated with the company of interest by typing in the name of the company. Then search for 10-K filings and find item 9. Item 9-A is a section labeled "Controls and Procedures," which is a good place to start looking at information on the internal control of the company.

Internal control is a key aspect in the reliability of financial reports. Fortunately, provisions of the Sarbanes-Oxley Act have focused attention on internal control over financial reporting. Companies now must assess the effectiveness of their internal control over financial reporting.

CHAPTER 24

THE AUDITORS' OPINION

THE AUDITORS' OPINION is part of audited financial statements and although it is not a guarantee, it provides a quality signal about the statements. Auditors can issue several different types of audit opinions, depending on the results of audit procedures. A qualified or adverse opinion is a warning sign that readers should investigate further to discover why the auditors did not issue an unqualified opinion. A disclaimer is no opinion, and the user of the financial statements should determine why that occurred.

QUICK POINTS: THE AUDITORS' OPINION

- ❖ An audit lends credibility to financial statements.
- ❖ Audits are required by the Sarbanes-Oxley Act and by the SEC for companies with publicly traded stock.
- ❖ An audit report can take one of several forms:
  - ❖ Unqualified.
  - ❖ Qualified.
  - ❖ Disclaimer.
  - ❖ Adverse.
- ❖ Signals in the audit report include:
  - ❖ Scope limitation.
  - ❖ Pervasive uncertainties.

What Purpose Does an Audit Serve?

Management is responsible for the financial statements of the company. The financial statements are the means by which investors, the owners of the company, get information on how the company is performing. Investors need this information because they can't be on-site watching to make sure the managers are doing a good job. The financial statements tell the owners about the effectiveness of management. The problem is that managers may not always act in the best interests of the owners. They may be lazy, foolish, or thieving. If that is the case, the managers won't want to present the clear and truthful information in the accounting reports because they'll look bad. They will want to hide their poor performance, waste, or the siphoning of company assets for personal use, and the investors won't trust the truthfulness of the financial statements.

A public accounting firm is hired to perform certain specified audit procedures, and then it issues an opinion on how fairly the financial statements reflect reality. The audit procedures monitor management's behavior. Management, knowing about the monitoring and fearing discovery of dishonest behavior, is motivated to act in ways that benefit owners, not themselves. The audit opinion lends credibility because the financial records have been examined and checked by an independent outside party. The audit signals a higher-quality set of financial statements.

Why Do Companies Have Audits Done?

Companies hire auditors to comply with regulation. The SEC requires audited financial statements for all companies that sell or are planning to sell stock to the public. Corporations issuing stock to the public must file form 10-K with the SEC, including the annual financial report with audited financial statements. In addition to SEC requirements, the Sarbanes-Oxley Act requires an audit report of internal control over financial reporting.

Non–publicly traded companies have audits, though, too. Often, private companies hire auditors because their bankers prefer audited statements. The need to comply with regulation drives much of the demand for audits.

What Is the Significance of the Different Types of Audit Reports?

The audit report, or opinion, can take several forms. The most common type of opinion is an unqualified opinion. An unqualified opinion consists of five paragraphs and opines on three things. The opinion states that the assessment of internal control over financial reporting done by management is fair, that the internal control over financial reporting is effective, and that the financial statements are fair and in accordance with generally accepted accounting principles (GAAP).

An unqualified opinion may have a fourth paragraph, called an *explanatory paragraph*. If the auditors are relying on the work of another CPA firm, an explanation of that situation requires a fourth paragraph in the opinion. If the company has been inconsistent in the application of accounting principles, that is explained in a fourth paragraph. The fourth paragraph is also used to explain the auditor reservations about the continued existence of the company, called a *going-concern problem*, or some other uncertain circumstances. Through the use of an explanatory paragraph, the auditors can draw attention to a situation that may not affect the fairness of the financial statements but is still important information for financial statement users.

A qualified opinion states that everything is fairly presented except for a particular item. That item may be a departure from GAAP or a limitation on the scope of activities the auditors were able to perform.

A disclaimer is an audit report that doesn't give an opinion. Auditors use a disclaimer if they are unable to provide an opinion. The inability to come to an opinion can be the result of a limitation imposed by the company or a limitation of the environment. If the auditors are unable to perform all the required procedures, they issue a disclaimer because of a scope limitation. Auditors will also issue a disclaimer if the company has "pervasive uncertainties" that threaten the life of the company. The going-concern issue can result in either an unqualified opinion with an extra paragraph or a disclaimer.

An adverse opinion is very uncommon because it states that the financial statements are not fairly presented. Usually the problem is resolved, and the auditors are able to issue another type of opinion.

What Signals Does the Audit Report Send?

The type of audit report and wording send a clear signal about the reliability of the financial statements. Most audit reports use very similar wording, suggested by the profession. Deviation from that wording indicates a potential problem. An unqualified opinion is the most desirable type of audit report. However, an unqualified opinion is not a guarantee that the financial statements are perfectly accurate. The precise wording of the last paragraph of an unqualified opinion is:

> In our opinion, the financial statements referred to above present fairly, in all material respects, the financial position of [company name] as of [date] and the results of operations and its cash flows for each of the years in the three-year period ended [date], in conformity with accounting principles generally accepted in the United States of America. Also, in our opinion, management's assessment that [company] maintained effective internal control over financial reporting as of [date], is fairly stated in all material respects, based on [identify controls]. Furthermore, in our opinion, [company] maintained, in all material respects, effective internal control over financial reporting as of [date] based on [identify controls].

An alternative would be for the auditors to express two opinions, one on the financial statements and one on internal control aspects. Either way, the phrase "in all material respects" means that the statements aren't perfect but are not materially wrong.

Audit procedures will not catch every error or fraud. The cost of an audit to detect all fraud and errors would be prohibitive because the auditors would have to check every transaction that happened during the year. Instead, auditors analyze the risks associated with the company being audited and sample transactions to determine the fairness of the financial statements. Most of the time this methodology works, but in some cases it doesn't. Most of the spectacular bankruptcies involved companies that had an unqualified, or clean, opinion in the year prior to the bankruptcy.

Any opinion other than an unqualified opinion signals problems of various degrees of seriousness. An auditor can issue a qualified opinion because another auditor was involved in auditing past years' financial statements. An unqualified opinion in this situation is not a problem and happens frequently in the case of mergers. The two companies were audited by different firms and the auditor of the newly merged company will have to rely on previous work when prior years' financial information is presented in the current year's annual report. No problem exists if the reason for the qualification is reliance on another auditor. But financial statement users should be wary of qualified opinions issued for other reasons, such as departures from GAAP, scope limitations, and uncertainties. Each of those can be much more serious.

A scope limitation indicates that the auditors were unable to perform one or more of the procedures required by auditing standards. Auditors may not be able to physically observe inventories or other physical assets due to their locations. Management may also limit what the auditors can confirm, such as accounts receivable. If auditors encounter a scope limitation, they must issue a qualified report.

Another reason for auditors issuing a qualified opinion is the existence of significant uncertainties. Significant uncertainties may be the result of litigation that the company is involved in. If the outcome of this litigation is uncertain and the scope of the litigation is significant or material, a qualified opinion would be issued. *Going concern* is a concept that means a company will continue in business indefinitely, that it is not in the process of discontinuing its operations. If the auditors feel that the company is not a going concern—in other words, it could go bankrupt in the next year—they will issue a qualified opinion.

Another type of audit opinion is the disclaimer. A disclaimer means that the auditor is unable to issue an opinion on the financial statements. Disclaimers provide no support for the fairness of financial statements, and investors should question why the company didn't hire auditors who were able to give an opinion.

The worst type of audit opinion is an adverse opinion. An adverse opinion asserts that the financial statements do not fairly present the financial position and results of operations. An adverse opinion is rarely issued because the company and the auditors usually work out the differences before that conclusion. Of course, an adverse opinion indicates big trouble.

The financial statements are prepared by the management of the company. Publicly traded companies must present audited financial statements. The key part of an audit is the audit opinion that tells readers whether the statements fairly present the financial position and results of operations. Knowing the different types of opinions will help you identify problems in your portfolio.

CHAPTER 25

CHANGE IN AUDITORS

THE SEC CONSIDERS it an important event when a company changes auditors and requires a special filing announcing the change. Although there might be a logical explanation, a change in auditors can be an indicator of problems.

QUICK POINTS: CHANGE IN AUDITORS

❖ When a company changes its auditors, it must file Form 8-K within four days of the change.
❖ Not all auditor changes are indicators of dire circumstances, and there may be logical explanations for the change:
  ❖ Mergers.
  ❖ Changes resulting from new regulations.
  ❖ Audit firm resource constraints.
❖ Many auditor changes do provide a warning about problems such as:
  ❖ Internal control weakness.
  ❖ Going-concern problems.
  ❖ Disagreements.
  ❖ Inability to rely on management representations.
  ❖ Audit scope issues.
  ❖ Illegal acts.
❖ Information on 8-K filings is available on the SEC's website.

What Are the SEC Regulations Associated with Auditor Changes?

The SEC requires companies that sell stock to the public to submit audited financial statements annually. The financial statements report to investors, who are the owners of the company, the financial position and results of operations for the year. The audit monitors what management presents in those statements, lending credibility to the fairness of the presentation. If a company changes auditors, either through company termination or auditor resignation, the investor needs information about the change to identify possible problems.

The SEC requires companies to file Form 8-K within four days of the change in auditors. On that form, the company must disclose who initiated the change, the company or the auditing firm, and the date of the change. The company also must state the type of opinion received on the statements in the last two years, including special identification of anything other than an unqualified opinion. The form should also report the board of directors' role and the audit committee's role in the change. The company must divulge any disagreements or reportable events. To prevent opinion shopping, the company must identify the new auditors, plus reveal any consultation with the new auditors regarding the disagreements or reportable events listed on the form. In addition, the previous auditors must agree or disagree with the information listed on the form. Beyond the disclosures on Form 8-K, companies are not required to explain the reasons for the change in auditors. They do not have to identify the specific reasons for the change.

What Are the Acceptable Reasons for Changing Auditors?

Auditor changes occur because the company dismissed the auditors or because the auditors resigned. Sometimes the change in auditors has a logical explanation. If two firms with different auditors merge, at least one of them will be dismissed. A merger is an understandable reason for an auditor change and one that does not signal problems.

The Sarbanes-Oxley Act imposed stricter rules on auditors of public companies. Firms that audit companies subject to SEC regulations must register with the Public Company Accounting Oversight Board. Some auditor changes occur because the audit firm decides not to audit publicly traded companies. Auditor resignation for this reason is another logical justification for a company to change auditors.

The third acceptable reason for changing auditors is related to auditor resignation due to resource constraints. With new auditing requirements spelled out by the Public Company Accounting Oversight Board, smaller auditing firms find that it is difficult to comply with the new procedures for all of their existing clients, given current staffing levels and expertise. Resource constraints are a plausible reason for auditor resignation.

When Is a Change in Auditor Cause for Alarm?

In some cases a change in auditors makes sense, but many times it indicates serious financial problems. Reading Form 8-K can sometimes reveal these problems. One alarm in the filing is a mention of an internal control weakness. A weakness in internal control can taint the entire financial reporting system in a company. If the internal control system is weak, the information on the financial statements can't be trusted. If the change in auditors coincides with identification of a weakness in internal control, the change signals a serious problem with the reliability of the financial statements.

A second alarm is the existence of restatements occurring at the same time as the auditor change. A restatement is often connected to weakness in internal controls. The controls didn't prevent some error or mistake, so the results of previous accounting periods must be corrected and restated. Restatements coinciding with auditor change mean some internal control weakness was unreported.

Form 8-K requires a company to disclose disagreements over accounting principles that it had with the previous auditors, even if those differences of opinion were resolved. A disagreement on Form 8-K is a third alarm because it suggests the company wouldn't follow GAAP. Auditors never push clients to deceive or commit fraud, so disagreement means that the company wanted to use aggressive accounting to manipulate the financial results. In the context of a change in auditor filing, it appears as if the auditors wouldn't agree to the company's demands and were dismissed. Auditors must also file reports about disagreements with clients with the SEC, making it unlikely that the company could hide serious disagreements.

A fourth cause for alarm is reporting on Form 8-K that the auditors cannot rely on management's representations. Auditors check the financial information that management prepares. If the auditors find serious problems that suggest dishonesty and fraud, they cannot trust the financial information that management provided. In addition to questions about the integrity of management, nonreliance on management may also mean that the audit committee and board of directors aren't effective. The inability to rely on management representations is a signal of serious problems with management and with corporate governance.

Scope limitations connected to a change in auditors is another serious cause for alarm. The auditors will request an expansion of procedures if they find problems. The company can avoid the additional investigation by firing the auditors and hiring another firm that might not be so thorough. Auditors change filings that disclose scope limitations, while rare, signal financial reports of dubious quality, and investors should beware. Form 8-K also requires the company to disclose illegal acts, obviously another warning signal of dishonest management.

Where Can You Find Information on Form 8-K?

Fortunately, the SEC's website has search capabilities that allow investors with an Internet connection to find information about filings. The website is at www.sec.gov. Click on the Filings and Forms (EDGAR) link and then click on Search for Company Filings. The first step is to find the company's Central Index Key (CIK), and there is a link to help you do that. From the Search for Company Filings page, you can search for Form 8-K filings using either the Companies and Other Filers link or the Full Text Search link. Both allow users to input the company CIK to retrieve filings. The full-text search allows the user to limit the search to a company and Form 8-K by using the advanced search feature.

A company that changes auditors is suspect. Although some changes are unavoidable, such as mergers or an audit firm resigning because it is no longer auditing public companies, most changes signal some problem. Particularly alarming are companies that change auditors often. Investors must investigate the reasons for the change to protect their portfolios. Research results indicate that companies that change auditors are at higher risk for litigation and a worse financial situation.

CHAPTER 26

PRO FORMA EARNINGS

COMPANIES WANT TO announce the good news about earnings at the end of a quarter. But what if the news isn't good? No problem. Companies can simply adjust the earnings number to get pro forma earnings.

What Are Pro Forma Earnings?

Pro forma earnings are calculations that depart from GAAP. Sometimes the departure really improves the usefulness of the

---

QUICK POINTS: PRO FORMA EARNINGS

- ✧ Pro forma earnings are measures of earnings that are based on methods other than generally accepted accounting principles.
- ✧ Pro forma earnings numbers have no common meaning and therefore are not comparable.
- ✧ Pro forma earnings go by many names:
  - ✧ Core earnings.
  - ✧ Operating earnings.
  - ✧ Economic earnings.
  - ✧ Earnings before interest and taxes (EBIT)
  - ✧ Earnings before interest, taxes, depreciation, and amortization (EBITDA)
- ✧ In December 2001, the SEC issued guidance on presenting pro forma numbers.

---

earnings number. For example, a company that rarely grows by acquisition makes an acquisition and has some unusual one-time charges. Removing those charges may help investors better understand the company's performance during the quarter than comparing it to the previous year that had no such charges.

Pro forma numbers become part of the marketing of the company. Companies usually present pro forma numbers in press releases shortly after the end of a quarter. At that time the official numbers, based on GAAP, aren't available. Touting the quarter's performance can increase stock price and increase the value of the company, a good thing for investors and the company.

What's So Bad about Pro Forma Numbers?

Pro forma earnings numbers have several problems. First, no common method for calculating them exists. Second, the pro forma numbers are released before the official numbers. Third, pro forma numbers never present worse results than the actual numbers. The problems of pro forma numbers make them unreliable.

Companies don't use the same formulas to adjust accounting numbers to pro forma earnings. No regulations govern the calculations. That means the company can adjust the numbers to make things look good. With no consistency in calculation, it is impossible for investors to do any meaningful comparisons from one period to the next for a single company's performance or a comparison among several companies.

The second problem with pro forma numbers is the time lag between the release of the pro forma earnings and the official earnings. Those adjusted numbers are released shortly after the end of the quarter, weeks before the official numbers. Then, later, when the official earnings are filed with the SEC, no one seems to pay attention to them. Companies aren't accountable for their adjustments.

The third problem is the bias inherent in the pro forma numbers. Pro forma earnings are never worse than actual earnings. It is always the other way around, with pro forma earnings presenting a rosier picture than the actual income numbers.

For example, in 1999, Trump Hotels released third-quarter results touting net income of $14 million after adjusting for a one-time closing charge of $81.4 million. The press release implied that all one-time items were removed to get to the $14 million income figure. But the results were even worse. The $14 million included a one-time gain of $17.2 million. Clearly, the company had picked which numbers to include in the pro forma earnings, and it depicted much better performance than the real number. The SEC found this so misleading that it issued a cease and desist order, to which Trump Hotels consented without admitting or denying the charges.

What Are Some of the Concepts Associated with Pro Forma Numbers?

Pro forma earnings numbers go by many names. All the names imply that the pro forma number is better because it eliminates items that detract from the usefulness of the earnings number. Common names for pro forma numbers include *core earnings*, *operating earnings*, and *economic earnings*. In each of these cases, the earnings number removes one-time charges to get at the earnings that will go forward.

For example, QUALCOMM's news release from 2000, shown in Figure 26.1, identifies the exclusion of one-time charges associated with the sale of its phone business. Many investors would disregard the one-time charge associated with the sale of that part of the business, so the pro forma earnings number may be considered more useful than the earnings based on generally accepted accounting numbers.

Some pro forma earnings numbers are commonly used by financial analysts. Those are earnings before interest and taxes (EBIT) and earnings before interest, taxes, depreciation, and amortization (EBITDA). These two pro forma numbers are used

Figure 26.1

News Release

Tuesday 18 April 2000, 22:30 GMT Tuesday 18 April 2000

**QUALCOMM ANNOUNCES SECOND QUARTER RESULTS
PRO FORMA EARNINGS PER SHARE $0.26**

Pro Forma Net Income Increased 74% From Second Quarter of Fiscal 1999—San Diego—QUALCOMM Incorporated (Nasdaq: QCOM) today reported pro forma revenues (see note below) of $649 million for the second quarter of fiscal 2000, an increase of 16 percent compared to $558 million in the year ago period. Pro forma earnings per share were $.26 in the second quarter of fiscal 2000 compared to $.18 per share in the year ago period, an increase of 44 percent. Pro forma earnings before taxes were $334 million in the second quarter of fiscal 2000 compared to $184 million in the year ago period, an increase of 82 percent. Pro forma net income was $207 million in the second quarter of fiscal 2000 compared to $119 million in the year ago period, an increase of 74 percent.

"During the quarter, we successfully completed the sale of our phone business to Kyocera. We also favourably settled a lengthy patent lawsuit with Motorola, resulting in the extension of its CDMA license to include QUALCOMM patents issued since 1995," said Dr. Irwin M. Jacobs, chairman and CEO of QUALCOMM Incorporated. "As expected, second quarter revenues reflected lower shipments in our chip business. However, we believe industry inventories have returned to normal levels and we expect a strong second half with record MSM chip shipments."

Note: Pro forma results for the current period exclude acquisition-related costs, including a $60 million one-time write-off of purchased in-process technology and $21 million in ongoing amortisation of goodwill and other intangible assets, $50 million in losses incurred by the exited consumer phone business and $56 million in charges related to the sale, $12 million in employer payroll taxes on employee non-qualified stock option exercises, $267 million in realised gains from sale of marketable securities and $3 million in other non-operating charges. Pro forma results for the prior period exclude the results of exited businesses and related charges. Pro forma earnings differ from reported earnings presented in accordance with generally accepted accounting principles because they exclude these cost and income items.

extensively and therefore have a common method of calculation, making comparisons valid.

What Are the Rules Regarding Pro Forma Numbers?

In December 2001, the SEC issued cautionary advice to companies releasing pro forma earnings numbers. The advice really consisted of five warnings. The first warning put companies on notice that the SEC did have the power to prosecute companies that misled the public with pro forma earnings. The SEC did just that when it issued the cease and desist order against Trump Hotels for the aforementioned misleading information.

The second warning told companies to clearly identify how the pro forma number was calculated. The SEC emphasized the need for details. It is not considered enough to just say nonrecurring or one-time charges are excluded from the calculation. The company has to explain the specifics and apply the same criteria when presenting comparative data.

The third warning was related to materiality. The SEC warned companies against turning a loss into a profit through pro forma magic. This warning emphasized that the pro forma earnings had to be not only literally true but also not misleading. That means clear disclosure of what is excluded and the amounts, so that investors can evaluate the validity of the numbers.

The fourth warning recommended that companies follow press release guidelines established by the Financial Executives Institute and the National Investor Relations Institute. Those guidelines don't eliminate pro forma numbers but suggest that the company include disclosures in the same press release about the deviation from GAAP. Some companies have interpreted this to mean that when releasing pro forma earnings, the company must also reconcile that number to the official counterpart number.

The fifth warning is to investors. The SEC reminds investors to be skeptical of pro forma numbers. In fact, it says, "Read before you invest; understand before you invest."

Pro forma numbers can be useful. Several commonly used earnings numbers have formulas that are consistently used to calculate EBIT and EBITDA, which makes those pro forma earnings measures comparable. Many other pro forma numbers change constantly. Companies are not required to use the same method of calculation from one period to the next. In that case, pro forma numbers are not particularly useful. Investors need to follow the SEC's advice and proceed with caution when using pro forma numbers.

CHAPTER 27

EXECUTIVE TALENT OR DECEIT

CORPORATE GOVERNANCE REFERS to the procedures in place to control managerial behavior. The goals are to ensure good, honest behavior and to protect stockholders. New regulations from the SEC and Sarbanes-Oxley assist in the achievement of these goals with a focus on business executives and on members of the board of directors.

How Do Regulations Protect Shareholders?

The Sarbanes-Oxley Act and other SEC regulations require disclosure of information, the institution of certain monitoring

---

QUICK POINTS: EXECUTIVE TALENT OR DECEIT

- ✦ The duty of corporate governance is to put in place procedures to control managerial behavior.
- ✦ Regulations such as the Sarbanes-Oxley Act help protect stockholders by ensuring:
  - ✦ Certification of financial results.
  - ✦ Reporting of insider stock sales.
  - ✦ Separate audit committees.
  - ✦ No personal loans.
  - ✦ Compensation disclosure.
- ✦ Boards of directors play an important role in monitoring executive behavior.

---

structures, and cessation of certain executive perquisites. These requirements help control executive behavior.

The Sarbanes-Oxley Act requires additional disclosures regarding executive knowledge of financial reports and regarding executive stock sales. The CEO and CFO must certify the financial results presented in the SEC filings.

Figure 27.1 shows the certification Hewlett-Packard included in its 10-K filing for the year ended October 31, 2006. This type of certification makes it difficult to use the ignorance defense that some executives have tried when charged with reporting fraudulent results. The Sarbanes-Oxley Act also requires more timely disclosure of stock trades by executives, including a prohibition on their trades during times when the pension fund is banned from trading. This provision is to prevent executives from profiting at the expense of other shareholders, as did the Enron executives who were selling their own shares while assuring the employees that their retirement savings were safe in Enron stock.

Figure 27.1

CERTIFICATION

I, Robert P. Wayman, certify that:

1. I have reviewed this Annual Report on Form 10-K of Hewlett-Packard Company;

2. Based on my knowledge, this report does not contain any untrue statement of a material fact or omit to state a material fact necessary to make the statements made, in light of the circumstances under which such statements were made, not misleading with respect to the period covered by this report;

3. Based on my knowledge, the financial statements, and other financial information included in this report, fairly present in all material respects the financial condition, results of operations and cash flows of the registrant as of, and for, the periods presented in this report;

4. The registrant's other certifying officer(s) and I are responsible for establishing and maintaining disclosure controls and procedures (as defined in Exchange Act Rules 13a–15(e) and 15d–15(e)) and internal control over financial reporting (as defined in Exchange Act Rules 13a–15(f) and 15d–15(f)) for the registrant and have:

   a) Designed such disclosure controls and procedures, or caused such disclosure controls and procedures to be designed under our supervision, to ensure that material information relating to the registrant, including its consolidated subsidiaries, is made known to us by others within those entities, particularly during the period in which this report is being prepared;

b) Designed such internal control over financial reporting, or caused such internal control over financial reporting to be designed under our supervision, to provide reasonable assurance regarding the reliability of financial reporting and the preparation of financial statements for external purposes in accordance with generally accepted accounting principles;

c) Evaluated the effectiveness of the registrant's disclosure controls and procedures, and presented in this report our conclusions about the effectiveness of the disclosure controls and procedures, as of the end of the period covered by this report based on such evaluation; and

d) Disclosed in this report any change in the registrant's internal control over financial reporting that occurred during the registrant's most recent fiscal quarter (the registrant's fourth fiscal quarter in the case of an annual report) that has materially affected, or is reasonably likely to materially affect, the registrant's internal control over financial reporting; and

5. The registrant's other certifying officer(s) and I have disclosed, based on our most recent evaluation of internal control over financial reporting, to the registrant's auditors and the audit committee of the registrant's board of directors (or persons performing the equivalent functions):

a) All significant deficiencies and material weaknesses in the design or operation of internal control over financial reporting which are reasonably likely to adversely affect the registrant's ability to record, process, summarize and report financial information; and

b) Any fraud, whether or not material, that involves management or other employees who have a significant role in the registrant's internal control over financial reporting.

Date: December 15, 2006
/s/ ROBERT P. WAYMAN
Robert P. Wayman,
Executive Vice President and
Chief Financial Officer
(Principal Financial Officer)

In addition to more disclosure of certification of financial reports and stock trades, Sarbanes-Oxley also requires the setting up of a separate audit committee composed of independent directors. The purpose of the audit committee is to hire the outside auditors and oversee the financial accounting process. All members of the audit committee must be independent, meaning they must have no ties to the corporation, other than being on the audit committee. Audit committee members also need to be knowledgeable about accounting and willing to accept the responsibility of monitoring a crucial aspect of the company. Audit committee members who are independent directors provide protection for shareholders. In the past, the CEO could appoint buddies to the audit committee who wouldn't question his or her decisions. Now that isn't possible, and investors can place more reliance on the monitoring done by the audit committee.

Regulations also provide safeguards to investors by requiring extensive compensation disclosures and the prohibition of loans to executives. New SEC executive compensation disclosures will come into effect in future reporting periods, but Ford decided to follow them in the 2007 proxy materials. The new disclosures include all forms of compensation and the dollar value of the noncash compensation. In tabular form, Ford discloses the total 2005 compensation for the top five executives. Then the total is broken out into salary, bonus, stock awards, options awards, and other compensation. The disclosure of the value of options is new information. Ford also presents comparative data for 2003 and 2004.

What about the Board of Directors' Role?

Members of the board of directors are supposedly elected by shareholders, but few shareholders take the time to learn about the nominees and make an informed vote and this results in a board packed with cronies of the company executives. CEOs would frequently sit on each other's boards, often on the compensation committee. The proxy statement lists each current board member, including some biographical information. Investors should read that section carefully to determine whether those directors will have the shareholders' interests at heart. Board membership is hard work, but directors receive compensation. The compensation is often in the form of a cash retainer plus some type of stock award.

For example, the 2007 Hewlett-Packard proxy includes this disclosure of director compensation:

2007 HP Director Compensation and Stock Ownership Guidelines

Employee directors do not receive any separate compensation for their Board activities. Non-employee directors receive the compensation described below. Each non-employee director is entitled to receive an annual cash retainer of $50,000 but may elect to receive an equivalent amount of securities in lieu of the cash retainer. In addition, each non-employee director is entitled to receive an annual retainer of $150,000 in the form of restricted stock or stock options (under special circumstances, the securities portion of the annual retainer may be paid in cash, but no such exceptions were made during fiscal 2006). The restricted stock awards are determined based on the fair market value of HP common stock on the grant date, and stock options are determined based on a Black-Scholes option valuation model. The restricted stock and options generally vest after one year from the date of grant, which is approximately one month after the annual meeting. Non-employee directors may elect to defer the cash portion of their annual retainer under the Hewlett-Packard Company 2005 Executive Deferred Compensation Plan. Under that plan, investment earnings are credited based on investment choices that are available to employees under the HP 401(k) Plan, and there is no formula that would result in above-market earnings or a preferential interest rate . . .

For that amount of compensation, even though board work is complicated and time consuming, shareholders can expect board members to be attentive and protect the interests of ordinary shareholders. A functioning board of directors is a vital part of the corporate form of business because it acts on behalf of all owners of the company.

GLOSSARY

Accrual Accounting: A method of accounting whereby a company recognizes revenue when it is earned and expenses when incurred no matter when cash was received or paid.

Adverse Opinion: An opinion given by the CPA firm after performing an audit on a company that states that the company did not follow GAAP and did not provide adequate disclosure.

Annual Report: A financial report published by a company once a year including the financial statements, notes to the statements, the auditors' report, and management discussion and analysis.

Asset: An item owned by the company that will provide future benefit to the company. An asset will appear on the balance sheet.

Audit: A process whereby a CPA firm examines and tests the information contained in the financial statements of a company. The CPA firm then issues an opinion on the fairness of the statements.

Balance Sheet: The financial statement that lists the assets, liabilities, and owners' equity of a company. It shows the financial position of a company at a certain date in time. Assets = Liabilities + Stockholders' Equity.

Capitalize: The process of increasing or creating an asset with an expenditure. The cost of the asset is then allocated over future periods.

Channel Stuffing: A method of increasing sales at the end of the period by encouraging customers to buy excess inventory with the promise of offering discounts.

Comprehensive Income: Net income plus other changes in owners' equity, except investments by owners or dividends.

Contingency: An uncertain future event in business. The outcome is dependent on some other event. (A lawsuit creates a contingency that will not be known until the lawsuit is settled.)

Credit: An entry in the accounts of a company. It is the entry on the right side of a T-account. (A credit reduces assets and expenses and increases liabilities, stockholder equity accounts, and revenues.)

Debit: An entry in the accounts of a company. It is the entry on the left side of a T-account. (A debit increases assets and expenses and decreases liabilities, stockholder equity accounts, and revenues.)

Deferred Income Tax: A balance sheet account that is the result of a difference between income tax expense resulting from GAAP and what is owed as income tax. It may be either an asset or liability.

Derivatives: A financial instrument that gets its value from some other asset such as the price of stocks, bonds, or commodities or an indicator such as interest rates.

Disclaimer: This is a type of opinion in an audit where the CPA cannot express an opinion. The CPA does not have enough information to issue an opinion.

Discontinued Operations: A readily identifiable segment of a business that has been sold or disposed of. The income from the operations of this segment and the gain or loss on the disposal are stated separately on the income statement as a nonrecurring item.

EBIT: Earnings before interest and taxes.

EBITDA: Earnings before interest, taxes, depreciation, and amortization.

Expenditure: A transaction that results in a decrease in the financial resources of a company.

Expense: A cost that has expired or been incurred. An expense reduces net income.

Factoring: When accounts receivable are sold to another party. The receivables are usually sold at a discount because they are sold without recourse, meaning the buyer bears the risk of nonpayment.

FASB: Financial Accounting Standards Board. The SEC has given this body authority to develop generally accepted accounting principles (GAAP).

Financing Activities: A section on the Statement of Cash Flows that shows cash inflows and outflows from long-term borrowing, repayment of that principal, the sale of stock, the purchase of treasury stock, and the payment of dividends.

Gains: The difference between the selling price of an asset and its carrying value on the books when the asset is not part of the normal business operations of the company.

Going Concern: The assumption that a company is going to stay in business for the foreseeable future.

Goodwill: An intangible asset that is generated when one company buys another company and the purchase price is greater than the fair market value of the net assets.

Hedging: Arranging a contract to buy or sell a commodity that offsets the potential change on other contracts from an economic outcome.

Historical Cost: The original cost of an asset, including the purchase price and all costs incurred in getting the asset into a usable state. This is an objective cost.

Income Statement: The financial statement that lists the revenues and expenses of a company for a certain period of time. Revenues – Expenses = Net Income.

Installment Sales Method: A method of revenue recognition whereby the profit on the sale is not recognized until payment is received. This method is used when collection is uncertain.

Intangible Assets: An asset that has no physical properties but gives the company value. Examples are goodwill, trademarks, and copyrights.

Internal Control System: Policies and procedures in a company designed to safeguard the company's assets and the reliability of its records.

Investing Activities: A section on the Statement of Cash Flows that shows cash inflows and outflows that are a result of changes in noncurrent assets such as investments, property, plant and equipment, and intangible assets.

Liabilities: A debt or obligation of a company that will be satisfied by the use of assets or by providing a service.

Management Discussion and Analysis (MD&A): A section of a company's annual report and Form 10-K that is required by the SEC. In this section, management must give readers information and explanations on liquidity, capital resources, and operations.

Matching Principle: A principle that requires that all expenses incurred to generate revenue in a period need to be recognized in that same period.

Notes to the Financial Statements: Additional information in the financial statements that describes the company's accounting policies, provides more detail on specific numbers included in the statements, and presents other supplemental information.

Operating Activities: A section on the Statement of Cash Flows that shows cash inflows and outflows that result from the acquisition and sale of a company's product or service.

Operating Expenses: Expenses related to the normal activities of a business. They are listed on the income statement after gross profit.

Percentage-of-Completion Method: A method of recognizing a percentage of the revenue or gross profit on a long-term contract before the contract is complete.

Pro Forma Financial Statements: A set of financial statements based on assumptions other than historical facts. These assumptions may be made on future levels of income and investments to aid in the budgeting and planning process.

Proxy: A statement giving someone else the right to vote instead of the shareholder.

Qualified Opinion: An opinion given by an independent auditor after examining the company's financial statements through an audit. This opinion states that the company did not follow GAAP in some situation, did not provide adequate disclosure, or did not allow access to some aspect necessary for the audit.

Restructuring Charges: The expense that is the result of a company deciding it is going to restructure. The estimate of total expenses along with a liability need to be recorded at the time the company makes this decision.

Revenue: An inflow to the company from selling products or performing services associated with core business activities.

Revenue Recognition Principle: A principle that states that revenue should be recognized when a product is delivered or a service performed and cash has been received or collection is certain.

Sarbanes-Oxley Act: The federal act that created the Public Company Accounting Oversight Board to oversee auditors that audit publicly traded companies. This was enacted in response to the bankruptcy of Enron and WorldCom.

Scope Limitation: When an auditor is not able to complete an audit due to restrictions put in place by the client or due to restrictions out of anyone's control. This will result in a qualified opinion or disclaimer.

Securities and Exchange Commission (SEC): A federal agency created in 1934 to oversee all publicly traded companies.

Securitization: Pooling high-quality receivables such as mortgages, loans, or credit card receivables and selling shares to investors.

Special-Purpose Entity: A separate entity that is created by a corporation to take on a specific task. This allows the corporation that created it favorable off-balance-sheet transactions.

Springloading: When a grant date for a stock option is set just ahead of a planned announcement of good news or just after an announcement of bad news.

Statement of Cash Flows: The financial statement that explains the change in cash from the beginning of the year to the end of the year. It explains these changes through three activities: operating, financing, and investing.

Stock Option: An option to purchase stock at a predetermined price within a specified time period.

Strike Price: The predetermined price at which the individual who holds the stock option can purchase the stock.

Tangible Asset: An asset with physical properties.

Unqualified Opinion: An opinion that an auditor gives after auditing the financial statements of a company finding that the statements were prepared in accordance with GAAP and are fairly stated.

USING EDGAR

Overview of EDGAR

All U.S. public companies are subject to reporting requirements under U.S. federal securities laws. Under these laws, public companies must file with the U.S. Securities and Exchange Commission (SEC) a wide variety of information, including periodic financial statements, matters to be voted on at shareholder meetings, and significant company press releases. The SEC has over 100 forms that must be filed by companies and other individuals for various reasons, and they receive hundreds of thousands of filings each year. Most companies report this information electronically via EDGAR, or the Electronic Data-Gathering, Analysis, and Retrieval system.

The SEC maintains the EDGAR database. As of May 1996, public companies were required to submit most filings electronically using EDGAR. Certain documents filed with the SEC are not required to be filed electronically and thus are not available from EDGAR. Smaller companies may also obtain permission to file documents in paper format if electronic filing is too expensive. Nevertheless, the vast majority of SEC filings are available from EDGAR. In 2006, 90 percent of all filings were in electronic format. All EDGAR filings are public information, and anyone can access and download this information free of charge. Demand for this information is tremendous. According to the

SEC 2006 Annual Report, in 2006 there were 528 million queries of the EDGAR database.

SEC Forms and the Relevant Information They Contain

The SEC has over 100 forms that must be filed by companies and other individuals for various reasons, but there are a handful of forms that contain all the relevant information necessary to uncover fraud and protect your portfolio.

Form 10-K

The annual report on Form 10-K provides a comprehensive overview of a company's business operations and financial performance. The most important information found in Form 10-K is audited financial statements. This information is the most transparent representation of a company's true financial condition. Along with the financial statements, Form 10-K includes management discussion and analysis of financial results. The first section of a company's Form 10-K usually gives a good overview of a company's business and important factors facing the company as well as the industry in which the company operates. In addition, Form 10-K contains explicit factors that companies are required to warn investors about, which can be a useful starting point for spotting activity that might be detrimental to a company's shareholders.

Form 10-Q

Form 10-Q is a quarterly form filed by companies and basically serves as an interim performance update between a company's 10-Ks. Form 10-Q contains unaudited financial statements.

Form 8-K

Unlike Forms 10-K and 10-Q, Form 8-K is not a report filed at regular intervals. Public companies are required to file Form 8-K with the SEC to announce major events that shareholders should know about. There is a long list of events that are considered "major events" and thus are required to be filed on Form 8-K. Some of the most relevant examples are:

- Mergers, acquisitions, or spin-offs
- Unregistered sales of equity securities
- Changes in a company's independent auditor
- Restatement of financial results

Proxy Information: Form DEF 14A

Form DEF 14A is the definitive proxy statement to shareholders. A public company must file this form whenever it intends to have a shareholder meeting. Form DEF 14A gives the details of the business to be covered at the meeting, including any proposals requiring a shareholder vote. Because it is not feasible to get all shareholders together in one place to vote on these matters, companies send shareholders a *proxy card*, which is a ballot shareholders submit so that their votes are appropriately tallied for each proposal. Two important matters that all companies must submit for shareholder approval are the election of directors and executive compensation. In addition, annual proxy statements contain an audit committee report from the company's board of directors, which can be a useful tool for gauging the quality of a company's internal controls and corporate governance.

Insider Trading Forms 3, 4, and 5

A company's officers and directors are required to disclose all personal trading in their company's securities. Form 3 must be submitted upon initial acquisition of the company's securities, and also if a person owns the company's securities and subsequently becomes an officer or director. After the initial Form 3 is filed, Form 4 must be filed whenever the officer/director makes any additional transactions for the company's securities. Insiders must file a Form 5 to report any transactions that should have been reported earlier on a Form 4.

Forms Related to Securities Offerings

U.S. companies that offer securities to the public must file with the SEC extensive information about the securities. Filings related to securities offerings are known as *registration statements*, because the law requires that these securities be "registered" with the SEC. There are three main types of form that companies file.

Initial Registration Statement: S-1, S-3, and So On

When offering securities to the public, a company will file a preliminary registration statement with the SEC before all the details of the securities offering are finalized. This first draft is filed on one of several forms beginning with "S"—S-1 and S-3 are the most common. The first version of the registration statement is almost always a rough draft that is missing certain pieces of key information. There may be multiple drafts of the registration statement filed with the SEC before the document is finalized and the securities are actually offered. Because they are rough drafts, these preliminary registration statements on the S forms should not be relied upon for critical financial analysis.

Final Prospectus: Forms That Begin with "424"

When a securities offering has been finalized, a company will file a final prospectus with the SEC. This prospectus, filed on a form beginning with "424," is the final and complete version of the preliminary registration statement that was initially filed on an S form. When a company files a final prospectus, it certifies that all information in the prospectus is accurate to the best of its knowledge; as a result, information in a final prospectus is more reliable than that in a preliminary registration statement.

Free Writing Prospectus

A free writing prospectus includes additional material information related to a securities offering. The content of free writing prospectuses varies widely and can include information such as term sheets, charts, graphs, and other information relevant to the securities offering. Like preliminary registration statements, free writing prospectuses can contain both draft and final information. As a result, free writing prospectuses should not be relied upon heavily, but they may contain useful information not found elsewhere.

EDGAR Research Basics

Search Options and Their Pros and Cons

There are several different ways to search for public company filings using the EDGAR database. Some are better than others, but no single search method is perfect—each has its own distinct advantages and disadvantages. The good news is that performing a few simple searches should give you the information necessary to begin analyzing a company's activities and making sure it is operating in the best interests of its shareholders.

EDGAR Company Search

The EDGAR Company Search facility is the best search to use when looking for information on a specific company. Following is a brief summary of the fields in the EDGAR Company Search screen.

Company Name

This field is self-explanatory. To start searching for filings right away, just type a company's name into the Company Name field and click Find Companies. This is a quick way to find all SEC filings that a particular company has made. Unfortunately, finding a particular company using this search can be a complicated process, as discussed later on.

CIK or Ticker Symbol

CIK stands for Central Index Key. A company's CIK is a unique number the SEC assigns to each entity that submits filings to the SEC. Because a CIK and ticker symbol are much more unique than the company's name, searching by CIK or ticker symbol is usually more efficient than searching by company name.

File Number

The SEC assigns a file number to multiple filings related to the same matter. For example, if a company files a preliminary registration statement for its initial public offering on Form S-1, and then files a final prospectus on Form 424B4, both filings would be assigned the same file number.

State

Again, it's pretty obvious what this field is for. This is the state of incorporation of the company.

SIC Code

SIC stands for Standard Industry Classification. SIC codes are three- and four-digit numbers that specify a company's industry and type of business. When conducting general industry research, it may be helpful to search by SIC code. A full list of SIC codes is available from the SEC website at http://sec.gov/info/edgar/siccodes.htm.

Ownership Forms 3, 4, and 5

These are the forms a company's directors and officers must file when they make personal investments in their company's securities. Larger companies tend to have a high volume of these forms (sometimes over a hundred in a year), so it is usually helpful to filter out these filings if they are not the subject of research.

Full-Text Search

The full-text search facility provides the ability to search the text of SEC filings from the last four years. Full-text searching can be very useful for research on a topic that is not limited to one specific company. Using the full-text search facility is a lot like using an Internet search engine such as Google. This is advantageous in that a tremendous volume of information can be searched quickly. On the other hand, it may be difficult to refine full-text searches to return meaningful results. For example, if you are interested in learning more about how companies report retained earnings, a full-text search for "retained earnings" would not provide useful results. This is because these search terms appear in many places in several SEC filings, often where retained earnings are not even the main topic of discussion. The SEC has provided an extensive FAQ on the EDGAR full-text search facility on its website. This publication contains detailed information on using search terms and operators to get the most out of the full-text search facility as well as the EDGAR database as a whole. The FAQ can be found at: www.sec.gov/edgar/searchedgar/edgarfulltextfaq.htm.

Example Searches

My First EDGAR Search

This first example provides a starting point for finding company filings and is a good introduction to navigating search results and actual filings.

Example 1:   Find the most recent audited financial statements for Ford Motor Company.

Here, we are looking for Ford's most recent 10-K. Because we have a specific company in mind, we will use the EDGAR Company Search facility. As mentioned earlier, it can be difficult to locate a company's filings by typing in the company's name. This example illustrates why. Try typing "Ford" into the Company

Name field. The search returns over 100 results. Ford is a huge organization with numerous subsidiaries, many of which begin with the word "Ford." Evidently, all of these entities have submitted filings via EDGAR. Unfortunately, only the ultimate parent entity has submitted the information we want.

A much more efficient way to search for Ford's filings is to input its ticker ("F") in the CIK or Ticker Symbol field. Searching by ticker automatically returns the ultimate parent entity's filings.

Ford's filings will be listed in reverse chronological order. You can use the Form Type field to filter these results. Type "10-K" in the Form Type field and click Retrieve Selected Filings. To view the filing, click on the link "[html]" next to the report you want to view.

Navigating SEC Filings

The next screen lists documents that Ford has filed. Most SEC filings consist of a main filing document (always first document on the list) and several exhibits. Ford's most recent 10-K is no exception. Ultimately, some of the exhibits may be useful, but the best place to start is always the main filing document.

Many larger companies that file on EDGAR have built hyperlinks into their larger filings. These links provide a user-friendly way to navigate a very large (200+-page) document. At the very top of the main filing document, you'll notice a link to the table of contents. Click on that, and you'll be brought to the main table of contents. The links contained in the main table of contents will direct you to any section of the main filing document. Click on Item 6: Selected Financial Data, which contains summary financial information for each of the last five years. For more detailed financial information, click on Item 8: Financial Statements and Supplementary Data. Under Item 8, you will be directed to another part of the 10-K (Exhibit 15). This is a common illustration of incorporation by reference, which is a not-so-user-friendly feature of EDGAR filings that is discussed in more detail later in this appendix.

Relevant Sections of Form 10-K

For purposes of researching a company's results of operations and true financial condition, certain sections of a Form 10-K can be very helpful. Following are the main sections of a Form 10-K that may prove useful.

Item 1: Business and Item 1A: Risk Factors   If almost no information about a company's business and operations is known, this is a great place to start. Item 1 contains a basic overview of what a company does. Item 1A lists risk factors, which are factors that the company views as the greatest threats to its operational and financial viability. An astute shareholder would definitely want to know about these risk factors.

Item 6: Selected Financial Data   This section provides a high-level overview of a company's financial results, showing a simplified balance sheet and income statement.

Item 8: Financial Information and Supplementary Data   These are the detailed financial statements with accompanying notes.

Item 9A: Controls and Procedures   This section is where the company attests that it is able to prepare financial statements that accurately reflect the true financial condition of the company. It contains management's assessment of the company's internal control over financial reporting and should include or make reference to the independent auditor's report on management's assessment.

Item 11: Executive Compensation   In theory, Item 11 is where a company discloses information about how much it pays its officers and directors. In practice, many companies just include a reference to their annual proxy statement to shareholders (Form DEF 14A). See "Proxies" for a description of proxy research.

Item 13: Certain Relationships and Related Transactions, and Director Independence   This section is a place for companies to describe any related-party transactions in which they engage. Item 13 is similar to Item 11 in that it is a common place for companies to incorporate their proxy statement by reference.

Interim Financial Reports

Example 2: Find the most recent quarterly financial statements for Microsoft Corp.

Microsoft's Form 10-K is a great source of information about the company. Unfortunately, it comes out only once per year. Later in a company's fiscal year, quarterly reports filed on Form 10-Q can provide more current financial information. The best way to get the most current financial information for a particular company is to search for all of the company's forms 10-K and 10-Q. In this case, start by pulling up all of Microsoft's most recent filings by typing its ticker (MSFT) into the CIK or Ticker Symbol field of the EDGAR Company Search screen. Next, at the Company Information screen, type "10" into the Form Type field and click Retrieve Selected Filings. This will return all of Microsoft's filings on forms that begin with "10"— most notably, all 10-Ks and 10-Qs. Simply select the most recent filing on the list to obtain the most current quarterly financial information.

Proxies

Example 3: Find the most recent proxy statement to shareholders for Supervalu Inc.

Approach this research task like the previous examples. At the EDGAR Company Search screen, type in the ticker ("SVU") and click Search. Then, at the Company Information screen, search for the proxy statement using the Form Type field. Remember, the name of the proxy form is DEF 14A.

The proxy statement is a good barometer of a company's strategic initiatives, as all major corporate actions such as takeovers require shareholder approval. In addition, the proxy statement contains required disclosure regarding compensation of a company's directors and officers, which has been a point of scrutiny in light of scandals involving outrageous compensation packages for company executives.

Other Helpful Hints

Incorporation by Reference: Follow the Bouncing Ball

Companies are often asked to submit the same information on multiple forms. In order to reduce the volume of information that companies must file, the SEC allows companies to incorporate by reference. The premise of incorporation by reference is that a company can submit information in one filing, and then for any subsequent filings where that information is required, the company can simply direct the reader to the original filing, rather than providing voluminous information that has previously been filed via EDGAR. Although incorporation by reference reduces the filing burden for the company, it can complicate the EDGAR research process. When information is incorporated by reference, look for it in the exhibit index to the filing. Otherwise, if the reference is to a completely different filing, pull up that filing from the Company Information screen.

Amendments: Additions and Corrections

Occasionally, a company will submit an EDGAR filing and then realize at a later time that the information in the filing was inadvertently incomplete or inaccurate. When this happens, the company cannot take back or undo the filing. Instead, an amendment to the original filing must be submitted that explains the error or omission and provides corrected information. Sometimes, the amendment will contain updated information to replace only the information that was erroneous in the original filing. Other times, the company may decide to just use the amendment to start over completely and provide the entire original filing with the corrected information. At the Company Information screen, filing amendments will be denoted by "/A" at the end of the form type. When conducting EDGAR research, it is important to be certain that all information taken from filings is up to date, and looking for amendments to any filings will ensure the quality of the information gained from the research.

EDGAR Search Fields

Most EDGAR search fields look for an exact match only. As a result, spelling mistakes and incorrect search terms can seriously hamper EDGAR research. For example, searching for "Genreal Electric Co" at the EDGAR Company Search screen will return no results. In addition, EDGAR needs search terms to be exact starting at the beginning of the search field, so "Electric Co" will not return meaningful results either. By the same token, typing "K" into the Form Type field of the Company Information screen will not pull up a company's 10-Ks or 8-Ks. The good news is that if you are sure about the first part of a search term, you can still find what you are looking for. If you are experiencing difficulty in getting meaningful search results, try truncating your search terms. For example, search for "General Elec" in the EDGAR Company Search screen, or enter only "8-" or "10-" in the Form Type field.

USING XBRL

Financial analysis is a key tool in evaluating the performance of your stock investments. Most professional investment advisors calculate ratios using numbers from the financial statements. Then, comparing those ratios over time can give a good picture of how performance trends. Or comparing those ratios for one company to the same ratios for other companies in the same industry can help pick the good performers in the group. Or comparing the ratios to industry averages shows how the investment is stacking up against all the other companies in the same type of business.

Why is it that investors don't do the quantitative research necessary to closely follow the stocks in their portfolios? The formulas for the ratios are readily available in any textbook, on the Web, or in books like this one. The financial numbers to plug into the formulas are in the SEC filings obtainable in the EDGAR database. What is stopping ordinary investors?

The reason ordinary investors rarely do the numbers themselves is that the data-gathering process is so tedious. Professionals have access to expensive databases that do all the mundane tasks—locating the documents, finding the numbers in those documents, transferring the numbers to a form that can be used by computers to do the calculations. Commands within the database result in reports that help the professionals follow the stocks. This convenience has a high price of thousands of dollars a year, often beyond the reach of the ordinary investor.

Well, soon the difficulties inherent in using financial data will no longer be a problem for individual investors. That problem is going away, with the introduction of XBRL. XBRL is a way of identifying pieces of data in an SEC filing so that anyone accessing the report via the Internet can download the data into a spreadsheet and perform calculations on the downloaded data.

What Is XBRL?

XBRL, shorthand for eXtensible business reporting language, identifies numbers in the financial filings that companies submit to the SEC. It works in somewhat the same way bar codes identify different products in inventory. Each financial item in financial statements is given a data tag that identifies it. Then the software reading the codes, or tags, "knows" what the item represents and where it should go in a report. This coding allows the data contained in XBRL documents to be transported to other software packages for further analysis. Seemingly magically, the revenue number from the SEC filing will show up as revenue in an Excel spreadsheet. Just as incredible, the different expenses will appear in the spreadsheet in the right cells.

To accomplish this, the developers of XBRL had to create a taxonomy that sets up the bar codes so that all companies using U.S. accounting rules code the financial numbers consistently. For example, the companies must all use the cost of goods sold bar code, or tag, to identify the cost of goods sold in their financial statements for the system to provide the benefits for investors trying to make comparisons. Taxonomies must be reflective of both U.S. and international business reporting rules. In some cases, additional elements are necessary for specific industries that have unique pieces of financial data in their reports.

While the taxonomies establish the tags for individual pieces of data, currently the volunteers participating in XBRL filings are able to create extensions to the existing taxonomies. Extensions are new tags for data items that the companies create. The extensions will inhibit the standardization and comparability of the data. It would be wise for the SEC to limit the extensions once the system is required. If that isn't the case, the user would have spreadsheets with data, but no way to compare because companies are establishing their own categories rather than using common classifications.

The pace associated with XBRL is fast. In 2004 the SEC began evaluating the benefits of using XBRL for required filings. Two years later it initiated a voluntary XBRL reporting project that involved 17 companies, growing to more companies now. The volunteers agreed to file their basic quarterly and annual reports in the XBRL format. In return, the SEC promised faster reviews of those returns. The result is that the SEC is considering requiring all companies to file using XBRL. In September 2006, Christopher Cox, chair of the SEC, announced that the SEC would revamp its EDGAR system that currently houses text documents of all the SEC filings. The new system would accommodate XBRL filings or interactive data. That is a strong signal that eventually companies will file their SEC documents in a format that can be easily used by ordinary investors.

Initially, XBRL was somewhat limited. The taxonomies were devised to accommodate individual stocks and mainly the income statement and balance sheet information. Some work on devising tags for notes and management discussion and analysis is advancing. Progress is speeding along in other areas of disclosure, too. In March 2007, a taxonomy for mutual funds was announced. The tags will provide investors with a way to easily compare the special disclosures, such as fees and objectives, required of mutual funds. In June 2007, several hundred companies will submit executive compensation data in interactive form. The SEC seems to be determined to move to interactive data.

Luckily, the SEC has made it possible for investors to try using XBRL data. On the SEC website, investors will find the software necessary to work with the filings of the volunteers.

Following are the steps for accessing the data.

1. Go to the SEC's website located at www.sec.gov. That should get you to a page that looks like this.

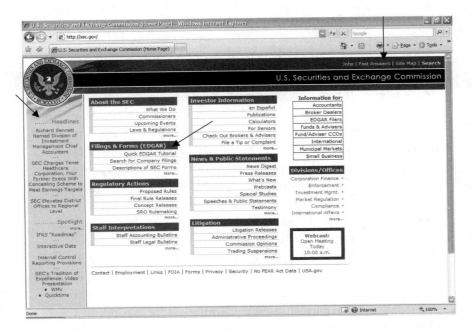

Notice that there are really three different parts to the screen. The first part is on the left-hand side under the seal. That area contains headlines and spotlights important initiatives of the SEC. The second part is on the blue bar just above the black bar that identifies the site as the U.S. Securities and Exchange Commission. That blue bar has job opportunities and three different ways to search the site for what you need. The third section of the website is the center part. That is where you start the process for using the interactive data.

2. Next, click on Filings & Forms (EDGAR) and this is the screen that should appear:

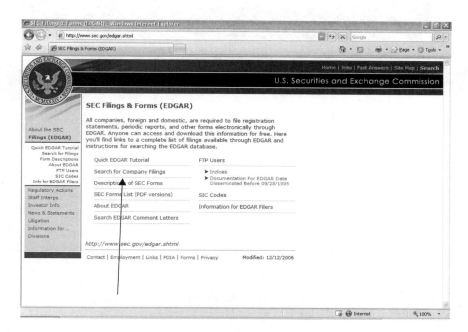

Notice that the column under the seal contains different content than in the first screen.

3. The next step is to click on Search for Company Filings and scroll down the page to the bottom.

Scroll down to view these options shown in the next screen.

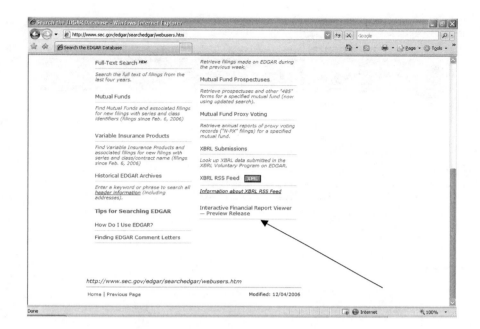

4. The last option in the second column is the Interactive Financial Report Viewer—Preview Release, and clicking on that link
   brings up this page:

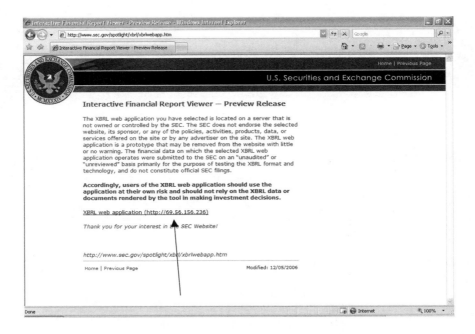

5. Click on <u>XBRL web application (http://69.56.156.236)</u> to finally arrive at the place where an ordinary investor can use interactive, or XBRL, data.

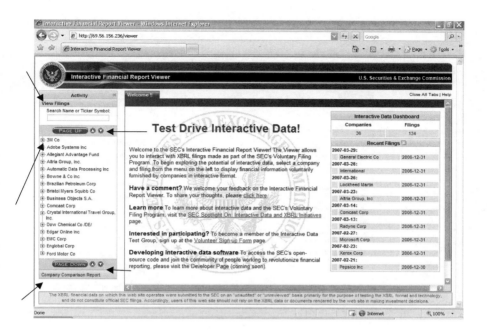

Again, notice that the page is divided into several sections. The left side of the page has two categories. View Filings (at the top) and Company Comparison Report (at the bottom) are two activities that the software supports. Click on Page Up or Page Down to reveal the entire list of companies with XBRL filings. Clicking on a plus sign inside a box next to a company name results in a list of the reports filed by that particular company. For example, clicking on the plus sign next to 3M gives you the following screen.

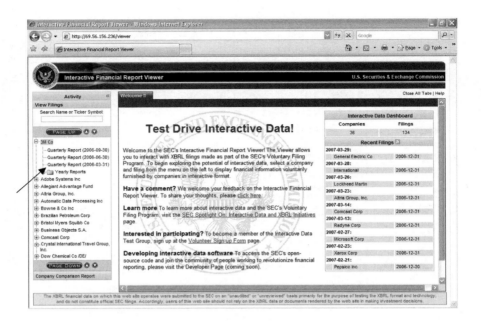

Clicking on a particular report results in a screen image of the report. A click on the Quarterly Report (2006-03-31) will result in this screen.

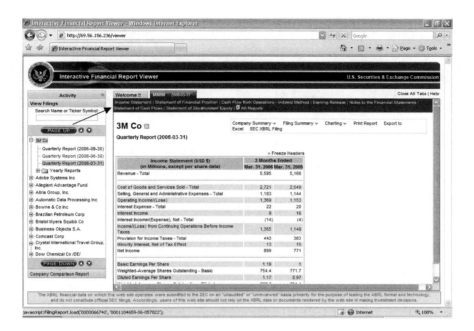

Notice the bar just under the word "Welcome." Listed on that bar are the reports available for the company. In the screen shot, you can see that 3M has many reports available for this filing date. If you point the cursor to a particular line of text in the report, a pop-up definition of that line item appears.

Directly across from the name of the company are capabilities other than those for viewing the financial reports. The Company Summary function provides the basic information including the company's tax number, ticker symbol, fiscal year-end, the state of incorporation, SIC code, SIC description, phone number, and address. The Filing Summary function displays information about that particular filing including the form name, the period end covered by the form, the form type, the filing date, the number of line items in the form, and the taxonomy used to code it. The Charting Function allows users to choose reports from several time periods and items on each of the reports. The software then prepares a chart displaying those items. Clicking on SEC XBRL Filing produces a pop-up window with the filings listed as you'd find them by doing a common company search. Clicking on the filing brings up the normal document without the special interactive features.

The Export function is a powerful one that allows users to export the data to an Excel spreadsheet. Clicking on that function brings up a dialog box asking if the user wants to open or save the result.

Clicking Save provides users with a copy of the spreadsheet on their computer. Clicking Open displays the spreadsheet, and users must save it to keep a personal copy. Either way, the result is a spreadsheet with the labels and numbers already loaded and properly labeled.

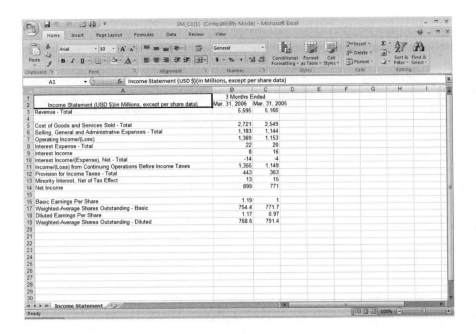

At this point, you can insert formulas to calculate the change from one period to the next of any of the line items in the spreadsheet. While the number of clicks is many, that path is easier than copying each of the numbers into a spreadsheet.

Instead of viewing just one company's data, the software allows you to do a comparison. Go back to the window that appeared after step 5, by clicking on the link to the preview software.

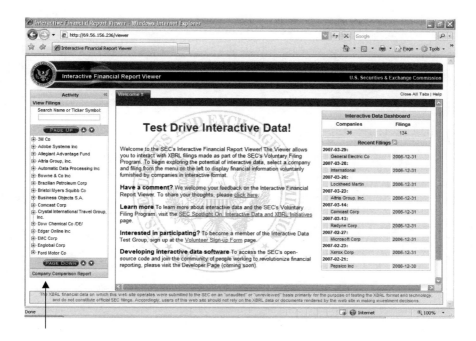

This time, click on Company Comparison Report, which is located at the bottom of the column on the left side of the screen. Clicking it brings up the following screen.

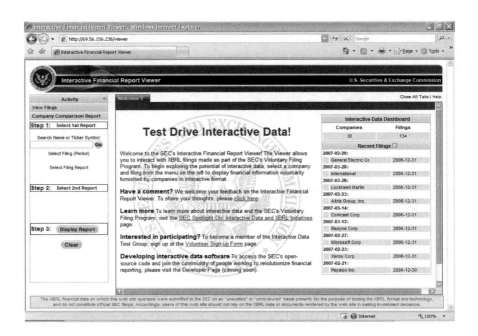

Now you can request data that compares one company to another. Place the cursor in the box titled "Search Name or Ticker Symbol." Typing the first letter of the company you are interested in produces a box with all possible companies with that first letter in the name or ticker symbol. Typing the letter "P" results in three suggestions. Pepsi and Pfizer make sense because those company names begin with the letter "P." The first suggestion, though, is Brazilian Petroleum Corporation, which starts with a "B." The ticker symbol for Brazilian Petroleum Corporation is PBR, and that is why it is displayed. You can choose the company by either company name or ticker symbol.

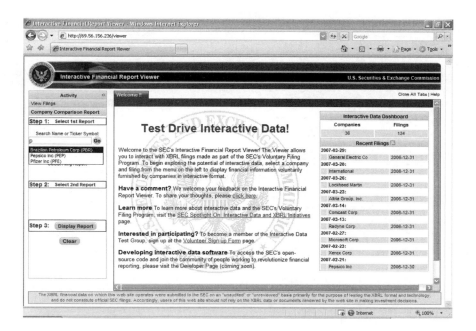

As soon as you choose a company, another drop-down box appears, in which you select the filing period. After choosing a filing period from the list, another drop-down box appears with the selection of reports available for that filing period for that company. In step 2, repeat the process for the second company. The result, after clicking on Display Report, will look something like the next screen.

To provide a wider viewing area on the screen for the actual comparison, click the double arrow. That closes the Activity window, allowing you to see more of the report. However, to see all of it, you have to use the scroll buttons.

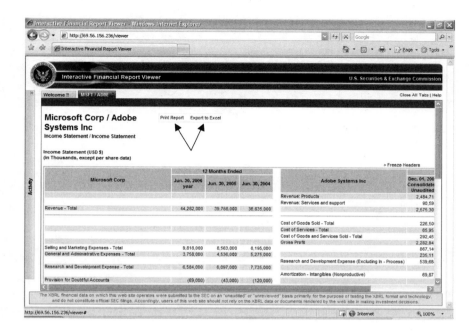

Notice that you can either print this report or download it into a spreadsheet. The spreadsheet that downloads isn't as clean as the single company view.

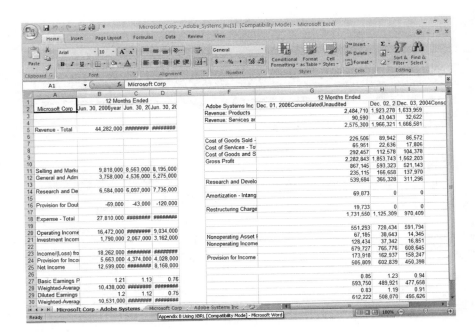

As you can see, the labels don't show up completely and instead of displaying numbers, some cells show ######. Both of these problems can be fixed by placing the cursor at the right edge of a column until a double arrow appears and then double-clicking. The column will expand to accommodate the widest data in the column.

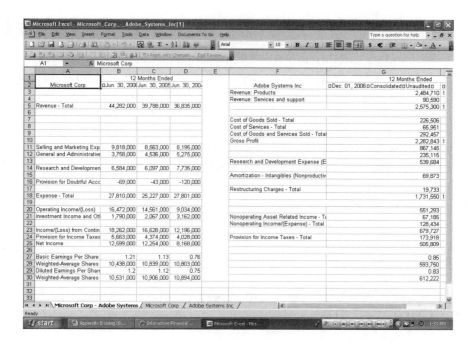

The structure of the spreadsheet is a combination of the two income statements, lining up items wherever possible. Notice that Microsoft's income statement is on the left-hand side and Adobe's is on the right. Columns for various years are across the top, and the labels for income statement items are in two columns. In some cases—for example, Selling and Marketing Expense—a label appears on the Microsoft side and numbers for each year presented are in the columns. On the Adobe side, no label appears but numbers for each year presented are in the columns. That presentation indicates that the label carries across both companies. For those items, a comparison is quick and easy.

A second presentation issue makes comparison more difficult. Notice that for some items, one company has a label and numbers and the other has neither. For example, Adobe lists Costs of Goods Sold—Total, Cost of Services—Total, and Cost of Goods and Services Sold—Total, but Microsoft has nothing for this expense. It seems improbable that Microsoft would have no Cost of Goods Sold or Cost of Services Sold. To investigate this, the user has to click on another workbook page, listed at the bottom of the spreadsheet. Clicking that tab reveals company-specific elements, and for Microsoft, that includes an item titled Cost of Revenue. For some reason, when Microsoft was coding the information, the company decided not to use one of the defined Cost of Goods Sold tags, but, instead, created a new tag that is company specific, naming it Cost of Revenue.

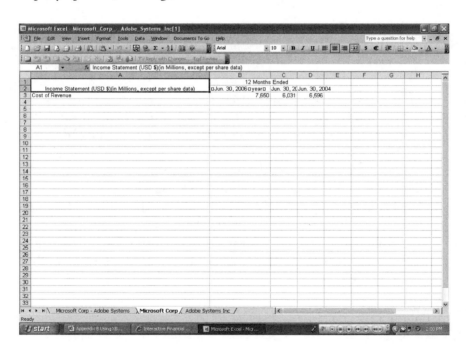

The presence of company-specific elements makes comparison more difficult for investors. They must do additional research to decide whether, in the Microsoft Adobe comparison, Cost of Revenue on the Microsoft income statement is similar enough to Cost of Goods and Services Sold—Total on Adobe's statement to do valid analysis. In some cases, like this one, it is an easy decision. The two elements seem similar enough to consider them alike in the analysis.

Once you've resolved the issues of presentation and company-specific elements, you can insert formulas to do comparisons. And that is the real power of XBRL. Even though it isn't perfect at this point, getting some of the data from SEC filings in interactive format provides ordinary investors with the tools previously reserved for professionals.

FINANCIAL FRAUDS/ SCANDALS

This appendix outlines some of the alleged financial frauds/ scandals that were brought to light in the years 2000–2002. These frauds were extensive in scope and dollar amounts. The information here gives a short summary of the alleged scandals, the chapter or chapters in the book where the issues were discussed, and the auditor for the company at the time of the incident in question. The summary only highlights the issues involved. More information on the companies and the charges brought against them or their executives can be found at the SEC website, www.sec.gov, or by entering the company name in a Google search. (Some of these cases have been settled; many ended with the defendants settling "without admitting or denying the Commission's findings.")

Company	Financial Scandals Chapters	Auditor
Adelphi 2001	Off-balance-sheet loans Chapters 1, 2, 17, 20, 21	Deloitte & Touche

Members of the Rigas family (founders of the Adelphi cable company) were the beneficiaries of multi-billion-dollar off-balance-sheet loans. These loans were used to purchase other cable companies, along with Adelphi stock. The company also overstated cash flow in 2001.

AOL Time Warner 1996 2000–2001	Inflated Sales Sold ads on behalf of others Round-trip Chapters 1, 4, 8, 9, 14	Ernst & Young

AOL Time Warner is alleged to have capitalized marketing costs instead of expensing them in 1996 when the company sent out computer disks. AOL is alleged to have inflated sales revenue by inflating the number of subscribers to keep the stock price up before its merger with Time Warner. AOL also inflated its advertising revenue by taking part in round-trip transactions with advertisers including Homestore.com.

Arthur Andersen   Shredded documents
                             Chapters 1, 23

Arthur Andersen, the auditor for Enron, shredded Enron documents and was accused of obstruction of justice. Arthur Andersen also was involved in a financial scandal at Waste Management, Inc.

Bristol-Myers Squibb   Channel stuffing   PricewaterhouseCoopers
2000–2001   Improper revenue
                             Recognition
                             Chapters 1, 4, 8

From 2000 through 2001, Bristol-Myers is alleged to have used channel stuffing to increase its sales and earnings by selling to its largest wholesalers and then covering some of the wholesaler's costs until the product was sold.

CMS Energy   Round-trip trades   Arthur Andersen
2000–2001   Chapters 1, 4, 8

CMS Energy engaged in round-tripping by selling energy to one company and then purchasing it back at the same price. This resulted in overstating trading volume and overstating revenues by approximately $5 billion.

Cendant   Inflated income   Deloitte & Touche
1980s–1998   Chapters 1, 4, 8

Cendant Corporation is the result of a merger of CUC and HFS Inc. Former CUC executives and directors were charged with instructing other employees to fraudulently inflate income. These executives then benefited from the increase in CUC and Cendant stock price by selling their shares of stock.

Citigroup   Off-balance-sheet loans   KPMG
                             Chapters 1, 2, 7, 17, 18

Citigroup aided Enron by setting up loans that helped Enron hide debt. Enron recorded the cash proceeds as cash from operating activities and not from financing activities. Citigroup also was involved with Dynegy Inc. in a similar scheme.

Computer Associates   Improper revenue recognition   KPMG
1998–2000   Chapters 1, 4

Computer Associates violated GAAP and recognized revenues before they were earned, to meet market expectations.

Dollar General   Improper expense recognition   Deloitte & Touche
1998–2001   Chapters 1, 5

Dollar General violated GAAP and delayed recognizing a significant portion of the $13.4 million in freight expenses, so that the earnings in 1999 would meet market expectations and ensure employee bonuses.

Duke Energy   Round-trip trades   Deloitte & Touche
2002   Chapters 1, 4, 8

Duke Energy was round-tripping by selling energy to one company and then purchasing it back from the same company at the same price.

Dynegy   Round-trip trades   Arthur Andersen
2001   Off-balance-sheet loans
              Chapters 1, 2, 4, 7, 8, 18

Dynegy utilized round-tripping by selling energy to one company and then purchasing it back from the same company at the same price. Dynegy was also involved with Citigroup in complicated transactions that were essentially loans to Dynegy but were characterized as cash flow from operating activities and not cash flow from financing activities.

El Paso   Round-trip trades   PricewaterhouseCoopers
2002   Chapters 1, 4, 8

El Paso was round-tripping by selling energy to one company and then purchasing it back from the same company at the same price.

Enron   Off-the-books partnerships   Arthur Andersen
2001   Bribed foreign governments
             Manipulated California
             energy market
             Chapters 2, 3, 7, 17, 18

Enron had off-the-books partnerships that were used to hide debt. Citigroup aided Enron by setting up loans to hide debt. The proceeds from the loans were shown as cash from operating activities and not financing activities. Arthur Andersen was charged with obstruction of justice because it shredded documents related to Enron.

Fannie Mae   Manipulated earnings
1998–2004   Chapters 1, 2, 4, 5

Fannie Mae manipulated earnings to smooth income by delaying the recording of both revenues and expenses in violation of GAAP. Earnings were manipulated to meet market expectations.

Global Crossing   Inflated revenue   Arthur Andersen
2002   Round-trip trades
                       Chapters 1, 4, 8

Global Crossing traded excess capacity on its network with other telecom companies.

Halliburton   Improperly booked cost   Arthur Andersen
1998–1999   overruns
                       Chapters 1, 4, 8, 9

Halliburton booked cost overruns on projects as revenue even though the company was not sure the customer would pay.

HealthSouth   Overstated earnings and assets Ernst & Young
1999–2002   Chapters 1, 4, 6

HealthSouth allegedly overstated earnings and assets to meet market expectations.

Homestore.com   Round-trip transactions   PricewaterhouseCoopers
2000–2001   Chapters 1, 4, 8

Homestore.com inflated its advertising revenue by taking part in round-trip/barter transactions with AOL.com and other advertisers.

ImClone   Insider trading   KPMG
2001   Chapter 1

Samuel Waksal, CEO of ImClone, along with Martha Stewart and others, sold their stock before the company announced that the drug Erbitux was not going to be looked at by the FDA.

JPMorgan Chase   Off-balance-sheet loans   PricewaterhouseCoopers
                       Chapters 1, 2, 17

JPMorgan Chase aided Enron in setting up off-the-books partnerships and essentially helped Enron hide debt from investors and creditors.

Kmart	Misrepresentation in	PricewaterhouseCoopers
2001	MD&A	
	Chapters 1, 19, 22	

Kmart executives did not fully disclose the company's financial position and financial difficulties in the MD&A section of the company's Form 10-Q for the third quarter of 2001.

Lucent	Improper revenue	PricewaterhouseCoopers
2000	recognition	
	Chapters 1, 4, 8	

Lucent executives engaged in improper agreements with customers. The revenue from these agreements was then recorded improperly or too early, in violation of GAAP.

| **Merrill Lynch** | | Deloitte & Touche |
| 1999 | Chapters 1, 2, 17 | |

Merrill Lynch was involved with Enron in transactions that overstated Enron's earnings. It effectively set up loans for Enron.

MicroStrategy	Improper revenue	PricewaterhouseCoopers
1998–1999	recognition	
	Chapters 1, 4, 8	

MicroStrategy was recognizing revenue early on the sale of software, in violation of GAAP.

Parmalat	Overstated assets	Deloitte & Touche
2002–2003	Understated liabilities	
	Chapters 1, 6	

The Italian dairy company told investors that the company had repurchased approximately $3 billion in debt obligations with cash when in reality the debt obligations were still outstanding.

| **Peregrine Systems** | Overstating revenues | Arthur Andersen |
| 2000–2002 | Chapters 1, 2, 4, 8 | |

Peregrine entered into false sales arrangements with resellers of its software. Peregrine improperly recorded revenue from these arrangements and then sold the receivables resulting from these false sales.

PNC Financial   Understated liabilities   Ernst & Young
Services   Chapters 1, 2, 6, 15, 17
2001

PNC moved loans from its financial statements to three special-purpose entities. According to GAAP, these special-purpose entities should have been consolidated on PNC's financial statements.

Qwest   Round-trip trades   Arthur Andersen
Communications   Chapters 1, 4, 8
International
1999–2002

Qwest traded excess capacity on its network with other telecom companies. Qwest also sold equipment and recorded the sales as revenue.

Reliant Energy   Round-trip trades   Deloitte & Touche
1999   Chapters 1, 4, 8

Reliant Energy was round-tripping by selling energy to one company and then purchasing it back from the same company at the same price.

Rite Aid   Overstated earnings   KPMG
1997–1999   Chapters 1, 5, 6, 9

Rite Aid overstated earnings through numerous fraudulent activities, including but not limited to failing to record expenses, recording expenses in later periods, adjusting cost of goods sold and accounts payable, improperly capitalizing expenses, and falsifying minutes of a finance committee meeting.

Sunbeam   Channel stuffing   Arthur Andersen
1996–1998   Improper revenue recognition
                           Chapters 1, 4, 8, 9

Sunbeam took part in channel stuffing, recorded revenue in periods earlier than allowed by GAAP, set up cookie jar reserves, and was not forthright in its communications with outside parties regarding its financial stability.

Tyco   Insider loans   PricewaterhouseCoopers
1996–2002   Improper revenue recognition
                           Chapters 1, 4, 8

Dennis Kozlowski was the recipient of $120 million in insider loans. Tyco also overstated its earnings by incorrectly recording acquisitions that it undertook. Connection fees were improperly recorded as revenue.

Waste Improper expense recognition   Arthur Andersen
Management, Inc. Chapters 1, 5, 6, 9
1992–1997

Executives understated expenses, did not write off landfill projects that were not successful, created salvage values for assets that should have had none, and other fraudulent activities. Arthur Andersen, Waste Management's auditor, was charged with issuing false audit reports.

WorldCom Improperly capitalized   Arthur Andersen
2001–2002 expenses
 Insider loans
 Chapters 1, 3, 5, 9

WorldCom allegedly capitalized operating expenses, therefore overstating net income by $9 billion. Former CEO Bernard Ebbers was the recipient of $400 million in insider loans.

Xerox Improper revenue recognition   KPMG
1997–2000 Chapters 1, 4, 8

Revenue was recognized early, violating GAAP, thereby increasing earnings and giving Xerox the ability to meet forecasts.

INDEX

ABOUT THE AUTHORS

Kate Mooney, Ph.D., CPA, is a professor of accounting at St. Cloud State University in Minnesota. In addition to receiving many teaching honors, she was a G.R. Herberger Distinguished Professor in 2002. She is the chair of the board of directors for Lutheran Social Service Minnesota, the largest not-for-profit social service agency in Minnesota. In May 2006, Governor Tim Pawlenty appointed Kate to the Minnesota State Board of Accountancy, whose 10 members are responsible for monitoring the accounting profession in Minnesota, including standards of practice, education requirements, and disciplinary actions. She lives in Cold Spring, Minnesota, with her husband, Steve.

Kerry Marrer, CPA, is the director of undergraduate programs in the G.R. Herberger College of Business at St. Cloud State University. Along with her duties as director, she teaches introductory accounting classes at St. Cloud State and has served as an advisor to student clubs, including the Student Government Finance Committee. Kerry has an MBA from the University of Chicago and has worked for several public accounting firms. She lives in St. Cloud, Minnesota, with her husband, Jim.